REGULATING UTILITIES:
THE WAY FORWARD

Professor Colin Robinson • Professor Colin Mayer
David Starkie • Professor Martin Cave
Professor John Kay • Dr Dieter Helm
Dr Stephen Glaister • Professor M. E. Beesley

With Commentaries by
Sir James McKinnon • Ian Byatt
Rt Hon Christopher Chataway • William Wigglesworth
Professor Stephen Littlechild • Sir Christopher Foster
Sir Sydney Lipworth

Introduced and edited by
Professor M. E. Beesley

Institute of Economic Affairs
in association with the
London Business School
1994

First published in July 1994

by

THE INSTITUTE OF ECONOMIC AFFAIRS
2 Lord North Street, Westminster, London, SW1P 3LB

in association with the
London Business School

© The Institute of Economic Affairs and M.E. Beesley 1994

IEA Readings 41
All rights reserved

ISSN 0305-814X
ISBN 0-255 36337-0

Printed in Great Britain by
Bourne Press, Bournemouth, Dorset

Text set in Times Roman 11 on 12 point

CONTENTS

INTRODUCTION

Professor M.E. Beesley
London Business School

THE THIRD LBS REGULATION LECTURE SERIES, again spon-
sored by the IEA, was held in the Autumn of 1993. It carried on the
traditions of the first two series. Once again, the main privatised
utilities, telephones, gas, water, electricity and airports, were in focus.
Railways joined the list, and, as in the first two years, topics of general
concern for the generalist as opposed to the specialist regulators were
addressed. It was the turn of academics to present papers, with the
major practitioners in each area taking the chair and commenting on the
papers.

The essential concerns of the specialist regulators, following privatisation, have had a consistent theme, though with varying emphasis in
each case: how to regulate natural monopoly; how to separate natural
monopoly interests from those open to competition; and how to enable
competition to emerge against what is usually a dominant starting position for an incumbent. Undoubtedly the main development in 1993 was
MMC's report on Gas, which made what most professionals regarded
as important contributions to each of these tasks. At the time of **Colin
Robinson**'s lecture, the President of the Board of Trade's decision on
the Report was not known. The President did not follow Colin's
support for the MMC's recommendation for divestment; but by accepting the MMC's insistence on full separation of the natural monopoly
from the rest of activities, and by bringing forward the date at which
franchise limits would be lowered, he did significantly forward Colin's
views of the necessary conditions for a swift transformation to competitive trading over gas networks. As **Sir James McKinnon** says, in
defining the 'extremely stringent' conditions for the separation, MMC
found a better solution than he had in mind.

Natural monopoly issues are most dominant in water. **Colin Mayer**
provides an approving appraisal of the track record of the operation and
regulation of the water industry so far. He argues that tough problems

remain with the UK price cap approach, notably of establishing consumers' trade-offs between quality of water and price; how to deal with unexpected efficiency gains in the companies' rewards, and how to use comparative data from the regulated companies. But he is confident that these will be solved with an appropriate technical input. **Ian Byatt** is perhaps less certain about the latter; he is wary of pinning down the regulators' functions in fine detail. Both are agreed on the importance of having the companies' shoulder the task of demonstrating need for expenditure.

David Starkie is also upbeat on *how* prices in airports are regulated – he argues that the basic separation of powers in the structure is sound. He is not a supporter of a 'super OFT' for all regulation. But he is critical of the CAA's remit and in particular the obligation to maintain the 'single-till' principle. Here, an intriguing inconsistency implicit in his paper emerges, namely between that principle and the pricing of BAA's London airports as they affect independent airports such as Luton. The rules simultaneously require non-subsidised prices for particular airports and adherence to the single-till principle, itself a source of subsidy. He also sees ahead some interesting problems on the issue of how regulating airports where capacity is constrained will impinge on airline competition. **Christopher Chataway**'s substantial contribution explains among other things how the CAA is dealing with the interairport pricing issue, and discusses how soon the single-till principle will raise conflicts which are still unresolved in principle. He is less optimistic than David Starkie about growing competition on routes until recently dominated by flag carriers.

Telecoms has the longest history of devising the terms on which newcomers can use the incumbent's network, though it is unique in the importance of simultaneous access to incumbents' customers as a condition for entry. **Martin Cave** reviews the development of arguments on principles of, and that of practical issues in, interconnect in the UK. He points out that there now is prospective competition between technologies with different cost structures, and from older technologies now able to serve substantial markets outside telecoms. He argues that the division of competition between and within technologies is much more plausible now than it was in 1991, thanks largely to developments in 1993, in particular in interconnect rulings. A postscript describes a key determination, that between BT and Mercury. **Bill Wigglesworth** confirms the centrality of interconnect issues, but has a somewhat different view of the driving forces in entry, stressing the regulator's influence on risks and rewards facing would-be entrants. He rates rules for accounting separation rather more highly than Martin Cave does, but he is, like Cave, optimistic on the prospects for competition.

John Kay takes up the issues of principle in regulating networks, drawing his examples principally from telecoms and water. He is particularly concerned with applying the relations between average and incremental costs to network pricing, which for him constitutes the thorniest problem in setting access prices, commonly supposed to reflect chiefly economies of scale and scope, and a system's efficiency. He thinks economies of scale are not important in heavily used systems, while economies of scope are moderate in water and small in telecoms. Nor, apart from the legacy of over-manning, is inefficiency significant. The important problem, he says, is errors in accounting methods, which tend to focus either on a top-down or a bottom-up approach. Activity costing, based firmly on causality and the purpose of expenditures, is superior. The regulatory strategy to evoke proper information on these lines is not to allow payment for expenditures not so justified.

At this point, an Editor's apology both to John Kay and to **Sir Bryan Carsberg**, his chairman, is in order. The hoped-for tape of a lively commentary, which provoked much discussion, did not materialise. But it was agreed that John Kay's arguments will be closely studied by both the regulators and the regulated.

In electricity, there was separation in the ownership of the natural monopoly from the potentially competitive from the beginning. Debate now centres on the still imperfect development of competition in generation and the correct regulatory context in which to pursue it. **Dieter Helm** perceives the present to be an uneasy mixture of government influence and market forces, in which the leading unknown is the future of oil prices. He discerns a consistent regulatory policy to increase the number of competitors against government intervention in fuel markets but thinks that a pro-competitive policy will be insufficient. He looks to a firmer framework of energy policy, in which governments have to make key capacity decisions across fuels. His exposition of the history of prospects of 'fuel policy' make an interesting contrast with Colin Robinson's treatment; and he is doubtful about whether, so far, electricity consumers have gained much from price regulation. **Stephen Littlechild** defends the record of Offer's dealing with the RECs' purchasing contracts and his refusal to intervene in the initial, government-inspired 'regulatory contract' with companies. His main fire is directed at Dieter Helm's arguments for more planning and central direction, anticipating the line that Colin Robinson was to take later in the series.

He, too, is sceptical about whether market mistakes outweigh those of governments.

Stephen Glaister's paper on railway regulation was necessarily anticipatory; there is, as yet, no railway regulatory record to appraise. His is a detailed exposé of railway regulation's policy context, the proposals, the functions of the two regulators (the Franchising Director to ORR, the Office of the Railway Regulator); and the emerging pricing and contractual framework. Stephen's paper has, arguably, the highest ratio of information to text of any of the papers. He sees the principal potential conflicts and ambiguities to be government ambitions to manage the onset of the market, its management of large public expenditures on rail, and the dilemma, familiar in the history of privatisation, of a Government's seeking to benefit the tax-payer and the rail consumer at the same time. He is guardedly optimistic that, as matters go forward, benefits from the new régime will persuade the Government to intervene less in markets as they emerge. **Sir Christopher Foster** points to the tension between promoting competition for the franchises and the City's willingness to fund. For him, the principal reason for creating so many new businesses is to ensure that the Government's commitment to subsidy will be matched by better ways of defining, and lowering the cost of, services. His principal doubts lie in the motivation of the remaining public sector body, Railtrack.

My own lecture deals with the abuse of monopoly power by single firms, a subject taken up because, after the wide-ranging discussions following a Green Paper on the subject, it appears that relatively little reform is intended. I argued the case that tackling the problem is one calling for heightened deterrence, to raise the cost to incumbents of attempted forestalling of entry, including notably the possibility of triple damages to an injured party. The context must be one which retains the present advantages of MMC scrutiny by making an adverse MMC verdict a necessary condition for private action. **Sir Sydney Lipworth** puts forward a number of cogent arguments in favour of the Government's decision actually taken, essentially not to change the *status quo*. The reader must judge for himself or herself, which, if any, horse is to be preferred.

I am pleased to add that the series will continue in the Autumn of 1994. In keeping with what is now the custom, it will be the Regulator's turn to present papers. The topics already agreed promise a vigorous continuation of the argument recorded in the papers which follow.

London Business School, July 1994   M. E. B.

THE AUTHORS

Michael Beesley is a founding Professor of Economics at the London Business School, now Emeritus. Lecturer in Commerce at the University of Birmingham, then Reader in Economics at the LSE, he became the Department of Transport's Chief Economist for a spell in the 1960s. His work from 1980 to the present has centred on the issues of deregulation and privatisation in telecoms, transport, water and electricity. Much of this experience is reflected in his IEA/Routledge book, *Privatisation, Regulation and Deregulation*, published in 1992. He started the Small Business Unit at the School, a focus for entrepreneurship, and was the Director of the PhD programme from 1984 to 1990.

His widely known work in transport economics and telecoms policy has taken him to such countries as Australia, USA, India, Pakistan, Hong Kong, South Korea, Cyprus and many in Europe. His independent economic study of *Liberalisation of the Use of British Telecommunications' Network* was published in April 1981 by HMSO and he has since been very active as an advisor to the Government in telecoms, the deregulation of buses and the privatisation of the water industry. For the IEA, of which he is a Managing Trustee, he wrote (with Bruce Laidlaw) *The Future of Telecommunications* (Research Monograph 42, 1989) and (with S.C. Littlechild) 'The Regulation of Privatised Monopolies in the United Kingdom', in *Regulators and the Market* (IEA Readings No.35, 1991). He has edited both of the previous volumes in this lecture series, the second of which, *Major Issues in Regulation*, was published by the IEA as IEA Readings No.40 in 1993.

He has been a Visiting Professor at the Universities of Pennsylvania (1959-60), British Columbia (1968), Harvard Business School and Economics Department (1974), McQuarie, Sydney (1979-80). He was appointed CBE in the Birthday Honours List, 1985. In 1988 he became a member of the Monopolies and Mergers Commission. He is currently Economic Adviser to Offer, the Office of Electricity Regulation.

Martin Cave is Professor of Economics at Brunel University. He was educated at the University of Oxford and worked as a Research Fellow in the Centre for Russian and East European Studies at Birmingham, before going to Brunel. He has been a Visiting Professor at the University of Virginia and a Visiting Fellow at the Australian National University and La Trobe University. Much of his early work was in economic planning; this includes *Computers and Economic Planning: the Soviet Experience* (1980), and (with Paul Hare) *Alternative Approaches to Economic Planning* (1981). Recently he has worked primarily on issues of regulation, especially of telecommunications and broadcasting, and the measurement of public sector performance. He has acted as consultant to various government departments and regulatory bodies, and was an adviser to the Peacock Committee on Financing the BBC.

Stephen Glaister, PhD, is Cassel Reader in Economics with special reference to Transport at the London School of Economics. He was a member of the Government's Advisory Committee on Trunk Road Assessment and he has been Specialist Advisor to the Parliamentary Select Committee on Transport. He was a non-executive director of London Regional Transport from 1984 until 1993. He has acted as advisor to the Department of Transport on bus deregulation, and he developed models for the Department for the cost-benefit assessment of urban public transport subsidies. He has worked on urban transport evaluation for the World Bank. In December 1991 he published *Transport Options for London*, and in March 1993, *Meeting the Transport Needs of the City*, both with Tony Travers, with whom he also wrote *New Directions for British Railways?* (Current Controversies No. 5, IEA, June 1993). He has contributed widely to the journals and in books on transport. He is Managing Editor of the *Journal of Transport Economics and Policy*.

Dieter Helm is a director of Oxford Economic Research Associates Ltd. and a Fellow in Economics at New College, Oxford. His previous appointments include Research Fellow in Economics and Management, New College, Oxford, 1981-83, Lecturer in Economics, Queen's College, Oxford, 1983-86, Senior Research Fellow, Centre for Business Strategy, London Business School, 1987-88. He is a Research Associate of the Institute for Fiscal Studies, and was the founding Managing Editor (now an Associate Editor) of the *Oxford Review of Economic Policy*. He is Editor of *Energy Utilities*.

John Kay is Professor of Industrial Policy and Director of the Centre for Business Strategy at the London Business School. He was previously Research Director of the Institute for Fiscal Studies, and Fellow of St John's College, Oxford. He is the author or editor of several books, including (with Mervyn King) *British Taxation System* (1978); (with Jeremy Edwards and Colin Mayer) *The Economic Analysis of Accounting Profitability* (1987); and (with Colin Mayer and David Thompson) (eds.) *Privatisation and Regulation – The UK Experience* (1986). For the IEA he contributed 'The Forms of Regulation', in *Financial Regulation – or Over-Regulation?* (IEA Readings No.27, 1988).

Colin Mayer is Professor of Management Studies, Deputy Director (Academic), School of Management, and Fellow of Wadham College, University of Oxford. He was educated at St. Paul's School; Oriel College, Oxford; Wolfson College, Oxford (MA, MPhil, DPhil); and Harvard University. HM Treasury, 1976-78; Harkness Fellow, Harvard, 1979-80; Fellow in Economics, St. Anne's College, Oxford, 1980-86; Price Waterhouse Professor of Corporate Finance, City University Business School, 1987-92; Professor of Economics and Finance, University of Warwick, 1992-94. Chairman of European Science Foundation Network in Financial Markets; Director of Oxford Economic Research Associates Ltd.; Associate Editor of *Journal of International Financial Management, Journal of Corporate Finance, Journal of Industrial Economics, European Financial Management Journal, Oxford Review of Economic Policy, Review of Economic Policy, Review of Economics and Statistics.* Honorary Fellow of St. Anne's College, Oxford; Fellow of the Royal Society for the Encouragement of Arts, Manufacture and Commerce. His publications include: (with J. Kay and J. Edwards) *Economic Analysis of Accounting Profitability* (1986); (with J. Franks) *Risk, Regulation and Investor Protection* (1989); (with A. Giovannini) *European Financial Integration* (1991); (with X. Vives) *Capital Markets and Financial Intermediation* (1993); (with T. Jenkinson) *Hostile Takeovers* (1994); articles in economic journals.

Colin Robinson was educated at the University of Manchester, and then worked for 11 years as a business economist before being appointed to the chair of Economics at the University of Surrey in 1968. He has been a member of the Secretary of State for Energy's Advisory Council for Research and Development in Fuel and Power (ACORD), and is currently on the electricity panel of the Monopolies and Mergers Commission.

He has written widely on energy including, for the IEA, *A Policy for Fuel?* (IEA Occasional Paper No.31, 1969); *Competition for Fuel* (Supplement to Occasional Paper No.31, 1971); *The Energy 'Crisis' and British Coal* (IEA Hobart Paper No.59, 1974); (with Eileen Marshall) *What Future for British Coal?* (IEA Hobart Paper No.89, 1981), and *Can Coal Be Saved?* (IEA Hobart Paper No.105, 1985); *Competition in Electricity? The Government's Proposals for Privatising Electricity Supply* (IEA Inquiry No.2, March 1988); *Making a Market in Energy*, IEA Current Controversies No.3, December 1992; and he contributed a paper, 'Privatising the Energy Industries', to *Privatisation & Competition* (IEA Hobart Paperback No.28, 1989). His most recent IEA paper is *Energy Policy: Errors, Illusions and Market Realities* (IEA Occasional Paper No.90, October 1993).

Professor Robinson became a member of the IEA's Advisory Council in 1982 and was appointed its Editorial Director in 1992. He was appointed a Trustee of the Wincott Foundation in 1993. He received the British Institute of Energy Economists' award as 'Economist of the Year 1992'.

David Starkie is a graduate and post-graduate of the London School of Economics. Apart from a two year contract with the Western Australian Government, when he served as Deputy to the Director General of Transport, he followed a mainly academic career until 1985 and was, latterly, Professor at the University of Adelaide. Since returning to the UK in the mid-1980s he has been engaged in full-time consultancy and in 1989 he joined Putnam, Hayes and Bartlett, the Anglo-American economics consultancy, as a Director. During his career he has served on a number of government committees and has advised various House of Commons' Select Committees since 1972. At the present time he is adviser to the House of Commons Transport Committee inquiry into UK-US bilateral relations in civil aviation. He is a Member of the Royal Economic Society and an Associate of the American Bar Association. He is the author of many books and papers including contributions to *Economic Affairs* and 'British Rail: Competition on the Network' in *Privatisation & Competition: A Market Prospectus* (IEA Hobart Paperback 28, 1989).

GAS: WHAT TO DO AFTER THE MMC VERDICT

Colin Robinson
Institute of Economic Affairs

ALTHOUGH MY TITLE enjoins me to discuss the gas market after the MMC's August 1993 report,[1] I begin by setting that report in the context of recent history. We need to go back about 30 years to unearth the roots of the problems which have come into the open since gas privatisation and which continue to plague the British gas market.

The North Sea and the Gas Market: 1964 to 1985

My survey of recent history begins just after the passage of the Continental Shelf Act 1964 which formed the basis for the subsequent exploitation of North Sea oil and gas.

Between 1964 and 1967 when the principal southern basin North Sea gas fields were discovered, the British gas industry was just awakening from its long existence as a rather sleepy supplier of high-priced gas manufactured from coal. New relatively low-cost methods of making gas from light oil fractions had only recently been introduced. But, as the scale of natural gas discoveries became clear in the mid-1960s, transformation of the industry began. For the first time, it had supplies of gas cheap enough not only to sweep the central heating market but to compete with fuel oil and coal in the industrial market. Between the mid-1960s and mid-1970s, gas sales almost quadrupled and virtually the whole country was converted to this new form of gas which had about twice the calorific value per unit of volume of the old 'town' gas.

In technical terms, the programme to introduce natural gas appeared successful. The large gas fields of the southern basin were brought into production quickly. Conversion of pipelines and consumers' appliances

---

[1] Monopolies and Mergers Commission, *Gas and British Gas plc*, Cm. 2314-2317 (three volumes), London: HMSO, August 1993.

was completed more or less on time, if expensively. The engineers who ran the nationalised gas industry were pleased with their achievements.

However, the gas market established in the mid-1960s had extremely undesirable features, the effects of which persist to this day. One fundamental error, in my view, was the government's unwillingness to auction off exploration and production licences.[2] One consequence of that initial decision to hand out valuable licences virtually for free was that governments gave considerable monopoly and monopsony power to the Gas Council and its successor, British Gas, in the hope that they would be able to collect the rent from gas production.

Effects of BG as a Rent Collector

The use of British Gas as a rent collector had unfortunate effects on both the supply and the demand sides of the gas market. Its monopsony power was such that the 'beach' price of gas in the early contracts (1·2 pence per therm, equivalent to about 10 pence per therm in 1993 prices) was very depressed. Consequently, exploration for gas in the southern basin of the North Sea ground virtually to a halt in the 1970s. Effects on the demand side are less clear because it is uncertain how gas prices in Britain related to what they would have been in a competitive market; but it is probable there was some over-stimulation of demand.

Moreover, as any organisation theorist would have predicted, the policy was ineffective as a method of collecting rent for government. Rent was undoubtedly extracted from the oil companies but there was no means of removing it from British Gas which consequently showed the symptoms of 'organisational slack'. If natural resource rent is to be collected from private companies (which is arguable) presumably it should go to the state not to the employees of a state corporation.[3] Belatedly, the government acknowledged the problem in 1981 when it introduced the Gas Levy in an effort to retrieve some of the rent from British Gas.

That is only the beginning of the story. The very powerful position in which British Gas was placed led it to behave like a textbook monopolist. Its access to cheap gas made it very competitive relative to other fuels and allowed it to penetrate most parts of the energy market, except for transport. Entry to the market by other gas suppliers was

---

[2] Kenneth W. Dam, *Oil Resources: Who Gets What How?*, University of Chicago Press, 1976.

[3] Colin Robinson and Jon Morgan, *North Sea Oil in the Future*, Macmillan, 1976, Chapter 9.

prohibited by the state so British Gas was not threatened. It had no incentive to hold down costs. Prices did not need to be cost-reflective so it indulged in averaging of prices. British Gas became possessive about 'its' gas, 'its' pipeline system and other appendages of power. Even though the corporation did not appear particularly profitable – partly because at times its prices were held down by government – there are, of course, less conspicuous ways of enjoying the benefit of a monopoly position than declaring high profits.

The effects of monopolisation and monopsonisation spread far and wide, reaching back into North Sea exploration and production where the benefits of competition should have been realised. The oil companies, which had initially been extremely unhappy with the gas contracts which had been more or less imposed on them in the late 1960s, gradually accommodated to the monopolistic régime.

In a trade-off for the low beach price, the companies had signed 'depletion' contracts in which they dedicated whole fields to British Gas which had an obligation to purchase all the gas from these fields under long-term (25 years plus) 'take-or-pay' contracts. Most of the companies would have liked to be able to market their gas direct to consumers. However, they had the compensation of knowing that any gas deposit they discovered which could profitably be exploited would eventually be contracted to British Gas. The present values of their finds were diminished by relatively low prices, long pre-production periods and comparatively slow rates of depletion. But marketing risks were negligible when there was a buyer willing to take or pay for whole fields.

As the oil companies came to accept the arrangement, gas exploration and production became *de facto* cartelised. Potential producers queued up for Department of Energy officials to offer them blocks to explore: under the 'administrative discretion' arrangements, blocks went to those the officials deemed most worthy. If they made a find, companies waited for British Gas to fit their gas into a schedule which ensured 'orderly' marketing of gas in Britain. A reasonably quiet life was enjoyed by all concerned.

'A Pernicious System' for Consumers

From the consumer's point of view, it was a pernicious system despite the technical success of offshore exploration and production and of conversion to natural gas. There was competition out in the North Sea – gas production had in effect been privatised in the mid-1960s since most of the discoveries were by private companies. But those companies were allowed to compete only to sell to the monopsonist. There was no market in the sense of a competitive discovery process which would have given incentives to producers to find new and better ways of satisfying the wants of consumers. The state ruled out direct access to customers except by British Gas, even though the oil companies could profitably have supplied larger consumers either through the British Gas system or through new pipelines. Everyone had to be supplied by a single 'public utility'.

Moreover, the state had to intervene to reinforce the system and to make sure there was no place where competition could break out. One outgrowth was a state trading régime of which Leonid Brezhnev would have been proud. The nationalised corporation, supported by officials in the Department of Energy, argued fiercely that foreigners must not be permitted to have any of 'our gas': evidently, no price could compensate Britain for such a loss. It was in order for British citizens to purchase gas from foreigners – but only if they were Norwegians, if all imports were made by British Gas so that order could be maintained in the British gas market, and if both governments were closely involved in the trade deals.

Then there was the awful possibility that one of the oil companies might bypass British Gas and sell gas direct to the electricity supply industry. Obviously, such a disturbance could not be tolerated. It could mark the beginning of a competitive market – because other large consumers might think a sale to the CEGB set a precedent for a sale to them – and in any case it would threaten the policy of successive governments of protecting the British coal industry by giving it a favoured position in electricity generation.[4] So an informal ban on gas sales to power stations was in force from the late-1960s onwards – long before the EEC thought of such a policy. The excuse for this absurd ban – which incidentally was partly responsible for the development of a highly-polluting generating industry – was that gas is 'too good to be burned under boilers'.

In pointing to the nature of the pre-privatisation gas industry, I attribute no blame to the industry's management. They were placed in a powerful monopolistic position by government and they acted like monopolists. What else would one expect? They were not alone. The state-owned electricity supply industry was production-orientated, technocratic and unresponsive to consumer demands. Indeed, British

---

[4] Colin Robinson, *Energy Policy: Errors, Illusions and Market Realities*, Occasional Paper 90, London: Institute of Economic Affairs, 1993.

energy policy in general provided benefits for producers and politicians rather than for energy consumers.

Gas Privatisation in 1986

When it became clear in 1985 that gas would be privatised, it seemed a wonderful opportunity to reform the old centrally-controlled régime in which a nationalised corporation and the government had suppressed any possible outbreak of gas-to-gas competition. Before long, however, it became obvious that the government was in an almighty rush to privatise gas to gather in the revenues (which turned out to be nearly £8 billion including loan stock). Because the government was in such a hurry to obtain the revenues it became very dependent on the co-operation of British Gas management which could obstruct any scheme it did not like.

It would have been possible, on privatisation, to have divided the corporation in a way which would have encouraged entry from the beginning. The scheme Eileen Marshall and I suggested[5] was for a separate pipeline company (state-owned, private-regulated or franchised) and a number of regional gas distributors based initially on the existing regional boards. Such a division would have encouraged oil companies with gas production in the North Sea to have begun direct supply to larger consumers via an independent pipeline network or by constructing their own pipelines. Competition in gas supply would thus speedily have been established. In time it would naturally have been extended to smaller consumers. Our scheme, however, would have made the whole of British Gas headquarters redundant: that was not at all what the senior management of the industry had in mind!

The Rôle of Pressure Groups

The story of gas privatisation is very similar to other utility privatisations. At the time of privatisation there is a coincidence of interests among all the powerful pressure groups which determine the form of privatisation.[6] The politicians, anxious to capture votes, want to raise substantial revenues and widen share ownership. They perceive that privatised companies with significant monopoly power are more

---

[5] Colin Robinson and Eileen Marshall, 'Regulation of the Gas Industry', Memorandum 13 in *Regulation of the Gas Industry*, House of Commons Energy Committee, HC15-i, London: HMSO, November 1985.

[6] Colin Robinson, 'Privatising the British Energy Industries: The Lessons to be Learned', *Metroeconomica*, No.1-2, 1992.

attractive to potential shareholders. Management wants to retain as much of its market power as it decently can, whilst reaping the usual benefits of privatisation in terms of higher salaries and increased 'perks'. The unions want to work for a monopoly, offering their members better terms. The City wants a monopoly to sell since it appears easier and more lucrative. No organised group has much interest in introducing competition.

Politicians will pay lip service to the idea of liberalisation but in practice they perceive its benefits as lying beyond any normal political time horizon. They find it much more convenient to leave the introduction of competition (which inevitably involves disruption) to industry regulators and the MMC. The principal task of these bodies, in all the privatised utility markets, has turned out to be the long and painful process of retrieving for consumers the benefits which could have been realised at the time of privatisation.

Gas is perhaps the most extreme example in the privatisation programme of how a small number of organised producers and politicians can triumph over large numbers of unorganised consumers. For the reasons given earlier, in 1986 British Gas management was in a very powerful position to influence the form of privatisation. Imbued with 'public service' ideas as they were, the company's senior managers did not want the corporation broken up. Moreover, they probably wanted to retain as much market power as they could. They succeeded in achieving such managerial objectives. British Gas was privatised in essentially the same form as its nationalised predecessor.

Although entry to gas supply was now possible, instead of being prohibited by the state, anyone wishing to enter gas supply in Great Britain faced formidable barriers. First, most of the commercially exploitable gas reserves found up to the time of privatisation were already contracted to British Gas: potential entrants would therefore have no substantial volumes of gas to sell for some years. Second, the privatised British Gas Corporation (hereinafter BGC) was an extremely strong and long-established incumbent with a large gas supply system, built up under state ownership, which offered security to potential customers as compared with an entrant supplying from a single gasfield. Thirdly, and crucially, BGC controlled the pipeline network which new entrants would have to use.

Creative Destruction, Entry and Pro-Competition Regulation

In these unpropitious circumstances, can a Schumpeterian 'gale of creative destruction' sweep through such an industry? The answer which is now emerging seems to be 'yes'. Although I have criticised the government's privatisation scheme, one must bear in mind the awful nature of the nationalisation régime which was its predecessor. Privatisation was a necessary act of government disengagement and a necessary (if not sufficient) step towards a liberalised market which lifted the prohibition on entry which had been the root cause of the evil effects of the old régime. Once entry is possible, the way is open for ingenious people to find and exploit the profitable opportunities which are bound to exist in a market which has just been freed after it has long been monopolised.

Pro-competition regulation has also had a very important place in accelerating the rate of liberalisation of the British gas industry. One of the consequences of emerging from privatisation with such obvious market power was that, as impatience mounted with the slow pace at which competition in gas supply appeared, BGC eventually brought on itself the full weight of a regulatory régime which tried to act as a countervailing force by stimulating competition. Both the company and the regulator have been unfairly criticised for the adversarial nature of regulation in the industry. But if government establishes a monopoly and, at the same time, sets up a regulatory office with the duty of promoting competition, conflict is the natural outcome of the pursuit by both organisations of their proper objectives.

A Consumer Uprising

After gas privatisation in 1986, events moved at surprising speed. The trigger was the increasing power of consumers. At the time of privatis-ation, the consumer voice was not heard (or perhaps not heeded). But, once privatisation was accomplished, the unholy coalition of interests which had secured an illiberal gas market dispersed. The politicians had gathered in their revenues and widened share ownership (and soon afterwards won a General Election); management was feeling satisfied with its retention of market power; the unions were happy that their members were working for a monopolist; the City had taken its commissions. But into the vacuum which had been created moved a new pressure group consisting of disgruntled consumers – not un-organised small domestic consumers, but large companies which had expected but had not received considerable price benefits from gas privatisation. They were potentially a very significant lobby, arguing that their competitive position was being threatened by BGC pricing policy.

The First MMC Reference

Remarkably, within only a year of privatisation, after complaints from such consumers that British Gas was abusing its monopoly position in the industrial market, it was referred to the Monopolies and Mergers Commission (MMC). The MMC's report in October 1988,[7] though not proposing any structural changes, made a number of recommendations intended to stimulate competition in the gas market. The three most important were:

o BGC should contract initially for no more than 90 per cent of any new gas field.

o It should publish a schedule of gas tariffs to contract customers and not discriminate in pricing or supply.

o It should publish rates at which it would be willing to transport gas for other suppliers through its pipeline system.

The MMC's objectives were to reduce BGC's monopsony power, freeing some North Sea gas for other suppliers; to allow entrants and potential entrants which wished to supply gas to large consumers to see what rates were being charged by BGC; and to provide access for those entrants to BGC's extensive pipeline network.

Action by the Regulator

More important than the 1988 MMC report, the Office of Gas Regulation (Ofgas), headed by Sir James McKinnon – and pursuing its duty to act in a way 'best calculated to enable persons to compete effectively' in the contract market – was from the beginning intent on easing entry into gas supply. The competition-promoting provision was, incidentally, only inserted in the 1986 Gas Act at the last minute by Michael Portillo MP (then a back-bencher), apparently because of his concern at the illiberal nature of the privatisation scheme. It turned out to be a very important amendment. *The Financial Times*, in a perceptive leader on 2 April 1986, headed 'Privatisation: a sorry chapter', said:

'The Government's other main concession was to accept a Conservative amendment giving Ofgas the general duty to promote competition in the

---

[7] Monopolies and Mergers Commission, *Gas*, Cm.500, London: HMSO, 1988.

supply of gas to industry. A fighting Ofgas director might make something of this...'

Indeed, Ofgas did. In 1990 it proposed that BGC relinquish its rights to some already contracted gas supplies in order to speed up the introduction of competition: the aim was that 1·2 billion therms a year (30 per cent of the firm contract gas market, excluding sales to power generation) should be supplied by BGC's competitors by 1993.[8] After some resistance, BGC offered to surrender to competitors 150 million cubic feet a day of gas. The gas would be available until October 1992 and would have to be repaid over the next five years.[9]

In addition, the new and potentially very large power generation market for gas, which emerged in the early 1990s as the government lifted the ban on gas sales for electricity generation and many Combined Cycle Gas Turbine (CCGT) plants were planned, was competitive from the beginning. North Sea producers were very keen to supply power stations direct and they quickly gained a bigger market share than BGC.

The OFT Intervenes

Then in 1991 radical proposals to enhance competition were made in a report by the Office of Fair Trading. The main proposals were that BGC should separate its pipeline and storage system from the rest of its operations, either by sale or at least by placing it in a separate subsidiary; that some of its contracted gas supplies should be sold to competitors; that gas imports should be freed; and that the prohibition on supply by competitors to consumers of less than 25,000 therms a year should be eased, with a new threshold of 2,500 therms a year for the 'tariff market' and possibly no limits at all after 1996.

The government accepted the proposed lowering of the threshold to 2,500 therms from 1993 onwards. BGC also gave undertakings to the Director General of Fair Trading in March 1992 that it would reduce its share of the non-tariff market (other than power generation and chemical feedstock use) to 40 per cent by 1995; that it would release gas to other suppliers so that they could supply the remainder of the

---

[8] *Regulating the Future for Gas Supplies*, speech by James McKinnon to NEMEX 1990, 4 December 1990.

[9] 'British Gas May Cede 10% of Market', *The Financial Times*, 31 January 1991.

market; and that it would establish a separate pipeline and storage unit with transparent and non-discriminatory pricing.[10]

Revising the Price Cap

At about the same time Ofgas agreed with BGC that, from April 1992 onwards, there would be changes to the price cap formula for the tariff market instituted at the time of privatisation. Not only was the X element in the RPI-X formula increased from 2 to 5, but the full pass-through of gas purchase costs allowed under the original formula (which gave BGC minimal incentive to keep down those costs) was modified.

Intrusive Regulation?

Despite its agreement to various undertakings and to the revised price cap formula, by the latter part of 1992 BGC was becoming increasingly concerned at what it saw as the intrusiveness of gas industry regulation. As I have explained, intrusiveness was inevitable, given the amount of market power BGC possessed on privatisation and given the regulator's duties. Had the government at the time of privatisation placed the pipeline system in a separate company and taken other measures to liberalise the gas market, regulation could have been confined to the natural monopoly sector of the gas industry (the network of pipelines) and it would have been much less adversarial. Consumers would have been protected by competition, and possibly by temporary price regulation for domestic consumers until competition developed in that market.

As it was, BGC was so concerned about the intrusiveness of gas regulation that, whilst negotiations were in progress about the rate of return appropriate to the BG pipeline network under threat of another MMC reference, the company itself decided it should refer the whole gas business to the MMC.[11]

Competition Increasing Before the Second MMC Report

I hope I have said enough to provide the essential background to the second MMC report which was published in August 1993. It came as the latest episode in a sequence of events which started with the monopolised and monopsonised gas market which lasted from the mid-

---

[10] *Gas and British Gas plc, op. cit.*, Vol.2, Appendix 1-2.

[11] 'Simmering Row Comes Into the Open', *The Financial Times*, 3 August 1992.

1960s to about the mid-1980s, continued with an ill-judged privatisation scheme in 1986 and then moved into a phase in which the regulator and the competition authorities tried to make up for the deficiencies of that privatisation scheme.

Pro-competition regulation certainly achieved some successes. In 1988 all supply to non-tariff consumers (the market open to competitive supply) was by BGC and at the time of the OFT report in 1991 BGC's share was still 95 per cent. In May 1993, however, BGC had only about two-thirds of that market (outside power generation): it was still the only seller of interruptible gas but competitors had 55 per cent of 'firm' gas supplies to the non-tariff market outside electricity generation. Another important development – though not directly attributable to the regulator – is that the old Soviet-style trade régime in gas began to change. Gas exports have begun from the Markham field to the Continent, there may soon be imports by organisations other than BGC, and a plan for a pipeline to link Britain to the Continental gas grid is well advanced.

The August 1993 MMC Report

The latest MMC report[12] is much more thorough and radical than the 1988 investigation. Depending on the government's reaction, it stands a good chance of clearing the logjam which had accumulated in the gas market. It was not simply that the regulator and the privatised corporation were at odds but that a thorough re-think of a misguided privatisation scheme was required. Whether or not one agrees with the details of the MMC's recommendations, it performs one of the functions at which the MMC is particularly good – prompting the powers-that-be to think about the future of a market and forcing them to face up to issues which they would prefer not to confront.

One major proposal is that British Gas should divest itself of its trading activities by 1997 (with accounting separation of those activities within BGC in 1994) to become an exploration, production, pipeline and storage company in Britain but no longer a trader in gas. 'Trading' on the MMC definition includes gas purchasing (including existing contracts), customer accounting, customer safety, marketing and some R and D. The MMC recommends that, prior to separation, BGC's non-tariff activities should be subject to market share limits and to the publication of price schedules. A slightly less onerous price cap would

---

[12] Cm.2314-2317, *op. cit.*

be applied: the present RPI-X formula for the tariff market would be adjusted from RPI-5 to RPI-4 from April 1994.

Under another recommendation, competition would be extended to smaller consumers than now because the British Gas monopoly would from 1997 be confined to consumers of less than 1,500 therms a year. It is estimated that about 400,000 homes and 100,000 businesses would thereby be brought into the competitive market. The report suggested that the monopoly could be abolished three to five years later.

There are also recommendations about the appropriate rate of return on BGC's pipeline network with which I do not propose to deal in this paper except to say that the MMC analysed the matter thoroughly. I shall return briefly later to the general issue of pipeline regulation.

The Government and the MMC Report

The Government is still deciding what to do about the MMC's recommendations. Its principal concern will, of course, be with the electoral consequences of its decision. It is not so much the job losses in this case which it fears – about 20,000 according to British Gas, or about 25 per cent of its present labour force, some of whom may find jobs in other supply companies.[13] Press reports indicate that Ministers like the idea of giving smaller consumers a choice of supplier but that they do not favour 1997 as a date for reducing the tariff market threshold to 1,500 therms a year because there might be a General Election then and the price effects are uncertain. Some reports, however, suggest that the Government might wish to abolish the monopoly earlier than the MMC recommended, perhaps to coincide with the freeing of the electricity market in 1998.[14]

Break-up seems less popular, partly because it would acknowledge openly something which is obvious but has not yet been admitted by the politicians – that the 1986 privatisation scheme was poorly conceived. Moreover, because it still has other privatisations to come (and also wants to sell its 40 per cent share of the electricity generators), the Government is no doubt nervous of accusations that it is perpetrating a fraud on shareholders who thought they were buying shares in a monopoly. The DTI, in its evidence to the MMC, was certainly very concerned to point out the difficulties of the break-up option. British Gas, however, no longer seems as anxious as it was at the

---

[13] 'British Gas Faces Break-up', *The Times*, 18 August 1993.

[14] 'Ministers May Hasten End of Gas Monopoly', *The Financial Times*, 25 October 1993.

consequences of a break-up. Indeed, it appears that the company has had contingency plans for such an event for some time.[15]

Is the MMC Report the Right Way Forward?

In considering the MMC report, there are three sets of issues which arise.

o *First*, should its major recommendations – to break up BGC and to reduce and eventually abolish the lower threshold which restricts entry to the small consumer market – be implemented?

o *Second*, if some such recommendations are implemented, what will be the place for regulation in the more competitive market?

o *Third*, if the market is made more competitive how can one overcome the problems which arise because it has been monopolised so long? Even though gas was privatised seven years ago, it still has all the trappings of a 'public service' system such as cross-subsidisation of consumer prices and transport charges and the assumption of social obligations by suppliers.

As space is limited, I shall concentrate on the first two sets of issues, commenting only very briefly on the third set.

Major Recommendations

Some form of vertical break-up of British Gas seems to me a crucial feature of any reform of the gas market. It is necessary to remove the conflict of interest, inherent in the privatisation scheme, of ownership by BGC (then the main gas trader) of the pipeline and storage system which potential competitors must use. Vertical division should greatly ease entry to the gas supply business. The MMC report put it rather well:

> 'BG is both a seller of gas, and owner of the transportation system which its competitors have no alternative but to use. In our view, this dual rôle gives rise to an inherent conflict of interest which makes it impossible to provide the necessary conditions for self-sustaining competition.'[16]

---

[15] 'British Gas Made Plans to Break Up', *The Financial Times*, 1 November 1993.

[16] *Gas and British Gas plc, op. cit.*, Cm.2315, Vol.1, para.1.6.

Nearly everyone who comments on the MMC's conclusions claims that removal of the monopoly of small consumers is the priority. I disagree. Break-up is more important, preferably along the lines suggested below. So long as there is the conflict of interest within BGC which the MMC identified, so long will the development of competition be seriously hampered. Moreover, there will be an awkward regulatory problem. The regulator will, as in recent years, have to try to supervise an organisation which is part natural monopoly, part not. The organisation will not want to provide the information the regulator wants and the problem of information asymmetry will arise. To minimise such problems the organisation should be divided so that the natural monopoly is isolated and regulated, and the rest is not. The organisations in the unregulated sector will have an incentive to contract with each other and to obtain whatever information is necessary to do so. The regulator will only have to deal with the natural monopoly.

Separate accounts and Chinese walls within British Gas would be no substitute for a break-up and genuine arm's-length relationships. BGC's competitors certainly would not perceive such walls to be effective and that perception would, in itself, constitute a barrier to entry. Failure to separate out the pipeline business at the time of privatisation was, after all, the crucial error which has hampered the development of competition; the opportunity should now be taken to correct that error. What is required is an arrangement which, in the MMC's words, secures the

> '...effective neutrality of the transportation system in such a way that this is in the interests of those who run it and that such neutrality can be readily perceived by shippers which find themselves treated...as welcome customers of the system, rather than simply as competitors in the supply of gas.'[17]

This neutrality is '...the principal condition for effective competition in all sectors of the market'.[18]

The logic of that statement does not, however, lead to the solution the MMC proposes – to turn BGC into an exploration, production, transportation and storage company, divesting the trading function. That route would still leave a conflict of interest: BGC would be a producer of gas and might therefore be perceived as giving preference to its own gas (about 17 per cent of UK indigenous output) in its

---

[17] *ibid.*, Cm.2314, para.2.100.

[18] *ibid.*, Vol.1, Cm.2314, para.1.9.

operation of the transport and storage system. The pipeline network is the means by which those who produce gas can reach those who demand it. How can competition flourish when one producer controls the pipeline?

Furthermore, a difficult regulatory problem would be perpetuated. Part of the 'new' BGC would have a natural monopoly element and would require regulation for that reason whereas part would not. Exploration and production are competitive and storage is potentially competitive also; it is only the pipeline operation which requires regulation on 'natural monopoly' grounds: the MMC would ring fence it within the new company. A separate regulated pipeline company (with the capacity provision and security functions which the MMC would give it) would seem a more logical solution which would concentrate the weight of regulation on those parts competition cannot reach and would remove fears of discrimination. There would be no question of preference being given to anyone's gas over anyone else's, so favourable conditions for entry to the industry would be created.

A Separate Pipeline Company?

Establishment of a separate pipeline company would attack the problems which have arisen in the gas market at their root rather than somewhat obliquely as under the MMC recommendation. The new British Gas (after divestment) would be similar to other North Sea producers instead of being the strange mix it is at present. BGC's current activities divide into four main functions (apart from appliance sales and international activities). One is upstream – exploration and production. Then there are the three downstream functions of transportation, storage and trading. For the reasons I have given, it would be preferable to leave the new BGC with the upstream functions of exploration and production and with trading, splitting off pipelines (from beach to consumer) into a separate regulated company. Better still, pipelines would be divided into several companies so that there would be some yardstick competition. Onshore storage and new offshore storage could be provided competitively. Both seasonal and diurnal storage provision could, in principle, be competitive activities despite BGC's claim that there are economies of scope in keeping transportation and transport-related storage in the same organisation. The offshore reservoirs (Rough and Morecambe) should probably remain with the exploration and production company.

The other main MMC recommendation – limiting and then abolishing the tariff market monopoly – is an essential change. Such a monopoly has no place in a privatised industry. The gas monopoly should be abolished at the earliest opportunity, though there may well be a case for phasing in the change, as the MMC recommends.

The Future of Regulation

If the monopoly over small consumers disappears in the course of time and there is vertical break-up of BGC, what place will there be for regulation in the gas market? Regulation has become such an integral part of this market that many observers seem quite unable to contemplate a future without it. The desire for regulation is to some extent just another manifestation of the lingering wish for a nanny state which tells people what to do.

Assuming that a much more competitive market in gas develops, there should be a corresponding decline in the scope and scale of regulation. Within a few years, there should be no need for price caps. Regulating a market which is actually or potentially competitive is not an additional safeguard for consumers but a recipe for stifling initiative and hampering innovation.

There will, however, be some regulatory functions to perform. *First*, pro-competition regulation will be required, at least during the transition to a more competitive market.

Second, the existing pipeline network will probably have to be regulated. The problem is that pipeline regulation poses some very awkward issues, such as the proper costs of and the appropriate rate of return on such an activity. Neither rate of return nor price cap regulation is therefore straightforward to apply. Consequently, it may be worth considering franchising the pipeline company or companies so as to introduce some competition. If competitive pipelines are built, that will also be helpful in demonstrating what costs should be.

Third, there will be demands to regulate the gas industry for safety, health and environmental reasons, especially since there are specific safety risks in gas. The intention of such regulation is well-meaning; everyone wants to be safe, healthy and have a clean environment. But, for reasons well-known to those who study the economics of bureaucracy, it tends to grow under its own momentum. Those who administer the system try to build empires. Moreover, they have strong incentives to play safe; therefore they push regulations towards the technological limits, secure in the knowledge that the costs will fall on others and that any victims will be invisible. Large companies, in particular, often welcome stringent regulations because they create barriers to entry. The answers to these problems posed by the growth of regulations go well beyond the scope of this paper. But in the present context, it seems important that most regulation which relates to gas is carried out by a gas regulatory office which has an over-arching duty to promote competition rather than by other regulators with no specific interest in the efficiency of the industry and the welfare of its customers.

So it seems to me the nature of gas industry regulation should change, moving away from price-cap regulation, concentrating on promoting competition and (where justified) standard setting. If the result is less regulation, that will be good news because regulation is always and everywhere so unsatisfactory. The fundamental problem is that, if there is no competitive market, regulators cannot know what to do: they have no standard on which to base their actions.[19] But if there is a competitive market, regulation becomes redundant. Systems and organisations, once established, have a habit of lingering beyond the ends of their useful lives. Let us hope gas industry regulation is not one of those.

The Legacy of Monopoly

Paternalism is a characteristic of nationalisation. British state corporations suffered from confusion between 'commercial' and 'public service' objectives. They performed functions, such as providing a safety net for the poor, which are more appropriately left to government (even if it does not perform them well). Privatisation inevitably reveals all the inconsistencies of pricing and charging of the old régime and price restructuring becomes a serious issue.

One of the principal relics, not just of nationalisation but of seven years of private monopoly in gas, is averaging of prices and charges. Consequently, though on average one would expect consumers to gain from the introduction of competition, there are likely to be some losers among those who had previously not been charged the full costs of their supplies. British Gas says that some small (and poor) consumers might find their bills almost doubled if they were charged full costs: according to its calculations, there will be six million winners and 12 million losers. That suggests BGC has been operating a most peculiar pricing policy but that is not the issue I want to address here.

---

[19] Israel Kirzner, 'The Perils of Regulation: A Market Process Approach', in his *Discovery and the Capitalist Process*, Chicago: University of Chicago Press, 1985.

A group of 12 independent suppliers has claimed[20] that its members could undercut BGC's present prices to domestic consumers by over 8 per cent on average whilst assuming an obligation to supply and all the service obligations which BGC now has. The group wants the domestic market monopoly ended by October 1996 and seems little concerned about whether or not there is any structural change to BGC. It argues that its members would operate under the same Ofgas price cap which applies to BGC so that there could only be winners. That is an interesting proposal which is worth putting to the test. There are, however, several provisos. The first is that the independent suppliers' proposal seems to make an assumption I would not care to make – that price-cap regulation will continue indefinitely. Second, it proposes a licensing procedure which will need careful examination by Ofgas (pursuing its pro-competition duty) to ensure it does not preclude further entry to gas supply. A continuing *threat* of entry is required for a rivalrous market.

Whatever one feels about these particular proposals, the interest which is emerging in supplying smaller consumers is very significant. No one can know in advance what prices might be in a competitive domestic market. But, in principle, it seems very likely that in a market so long monopolised costs are high, margins are generous and there is ample scope for new entrants to make a profit whilst providing lower prices and improved service to customers.

Summary

To summarise, my view of the latest MMC report on gas is that it performs the very valuable function of forcing politicians to look again at their 1986 creation – which resulted in private monopoly in the gas market after many years of state monopoly.

Removal of the monopoly over small consumers is very desirable and may even turn out to be popular politically. Break-up of BGC is also desirable: indeed, in my view it is the priority. If competition is to flourish in this market, it is essential that an independent pipeline company be established. As the MMC said, such a company would welcome customers rather than treating them as though they were undesirable newcomers to the market.

Although I have been very critical of government actions in the gas market, I think that in conclusion a more optimistic note is in order. Because of the efforts of the MMC and the regulator, there is now a

---

[20] *Wouldn't You Just Love to be in Control?: Competition, Choice and Value-for-Money Gas*, a report by the independent gas industry, October 1993.

genuine opportunity to move decisively to a liberalised gas market. If the Government takes action along the lines I have suggested – which would be a logical progression from efforts made over the last few years to break down barriers to entering the gas market – the outlook could be quite bright for gas consumers. Indeed, Britain's efforts to liberalise its energy industries, slow and hesitant as they have been, could by the late 1990s provide industry and commerce in this country with a genuine competitive advantage. No other major country seems ready to go as far in breaking down the state gas and electricity monopolies which for so long have dominated markets at the expense of consumers.

CHAIRMAN'S COMMENTS

Sir James McKinnon
OFGAS

COLIN HAS GIVEN US a very well reasoned and most interesting paper. He has covered the ground extremely well and very fairly. In my term of office a key rôle was played by the Monopolies and Mergers Commission (MMC). The first MMC Report in 1988 was quite critical. It broke the mould, in that it made reference to the fact that the monopsony would have to come to an end, as it recognised that natural gas was not readily available to competitors because of the way in which contracts had been completely taken up by British Gas. So, there had to be a timing point for competition, and price schedules to give everyone a reasonable opportunity to get exactly the same treatment as the next person. Now that does not mean that they were all treated fairly; they were just treated the same; but that was the start of the development of competition.

But there was one very interesting point at the end of the first MMC Report. It was to the effect that, 'If the measures that we have outlined prove not to be successful, we will require to come back and perhaps a structural solution will be required'. And that was the message that I attempted to draw to British Gas's attention, whilst I was hoping that they would make product available ahead of the proposed study by the Office of Fair Trading, which was due to begin in 1991. There was virtually no competition ahead of that. And so the MMC Report of 1988 cast its shadow ahead. In the event, OFT discovered that competition had not made the progress that had been hoped, that much remained to be done. It picked up the Gas Release Programme, bringing the monopoly in the domestic market down, amongst other fairly major points. Indirectly it propelled the industry towards another investigation by MMC. As Colin has said, it is a wide-ranging and thorough one.

I have to confess that MMC has come forward with a solution that was better than the one I had in my mind. I was obsessed with the thought of a completely separated pipeline system. My belief is that if you read the MMC Report carefully, you will see the terms and conditions that surround the proposed separation are extremely stringent. They almost amount to setting up a completely separate business. Now I believe that competitors will be interested in this in the sense that they can see the protection that comes from the MMC's proposals, giving the Office of Gas Supply very strong powers to regulate and keep prices of the pipeline system at a reasonable level to make sure that prices are transparent and even-handed. They need this to get into the market on the domestic side; and I think they will take heart from it.

But the important point is that this will be done quickly, by the speed of light compared with many other changes that have taken place. We do not require primary legislation. And so we can attend to the pressing problem quickly to allow the further development to take place in due course. 'Due course' is because there must be primary legislation even to take the trading side of British Gas away from the pipeline system. And it is for that reason that I support the MMC position. It is up to the Government now to open the final door by saying when, and at what stages, the monopoly in the tariff sector will be done away with. That is extremely important.

And the status of interruptible consumers should not be lost sight of. Competitors who have now made such progress in the firm sector of the industrial market will begin to take up a part of the interruptible load. Those moving into the domestic sector will also take part of the interruptible market simply by reference to the kind of load that exists in the domestic sector. All round, there is much to be said for development in the domestic sector which will read across to the industrial part of the market.

So my belief is that things are nicely poised. I would like to think that we would move towards a situation where there could be licences for competitors to take up in the domestic sector. I think that marches well with the fact that the regional electricity companies are in position, have shown an interest in becoming energy companies, have the infrastructure to deal with the large number of customers, and indeed have the desire to move forward as energy suppliers in a regional area. And this, I believe, will cause British Gas to compete because of the regional characteristic of the competition. They will compete regionally; hence the proposal that we made: 'You might as well get on with it now and break up the company into regions. That will speed the day whereby regional competition will take place.'

But in all of this, we talk of winners and losers. Some people may think they have lost; I do not believe there have been a great number of losers. The question arises from squeezing out inefficiency in the existing system. But the harder you squeeze, the more inefficiency goes, the better the opportunity is for those who participate in the market either as producers, suppliers or customers. There is some distance to go in this. The two elements that I believe will give a winning card to most people in this country are, first, to squeeze out inefficiency, and, second, to build the market, expanding the ways in which the product can be used.

2

THE REGULATION OF THE WATER INDUSTRY: AN INTERIM ASSESSMENT

Colin Mayer
University of Oxford

Introduction

THIS IS AN OPPORTUNE MOMENT at which to review the state of the water industry in England and Wales. We are now four years into privatisation and can therefore begin to develop a sense of the way in which the privatised industry is performing. In addition, the water industry is about to enter its first periodic review which will set the framework for regulation up to the next century.

The industry was privatised against a legacy of neglect. The Victorian heritage was more than showing its age. A serious lack of investment over the previous decades had left a leaking infrastructure which polluted rivers and beaches and delivered water whose quality was beginning to be questioned by customers.

Water privatisation was in part an extension of a privatisation programme which had already achieved the successful disposal of the telecommunication and gas industries. But in addition, the passage of EC directives on water quality and sewerage was creating a need for substantial capital expenditures. If the water industry had remained under state control these expenditures would have imposed serious burdens on the public purse. Privatisation was a mechanism by which a financial drain could be converted into a pot of gold.

Privatisation created 10 water and sewerage companies based on the old river basin water authorities. They joined 29 water only companies which were already in private ownership. The regulation of the water industry was divided between HM Inspectorate of Pollution (HMIP), the Drinking Water Inspectorate (DWI) and the National Rivers

Authority (NRA), which together are concerned with environmental regulation, and the Office of Water Services (OFWAT) which is concerned with economic regulation.

The Water Industry Act 1991 gave the Secretary of State the power to appoint water and sewerage undertakers and to impose conditions on their operation. The Licence specified these conditions and laid down the framework for the regulation of the industry.

Price Setting

Following the principles established in other privatised industries, the water industry is subject to price regulation. Prices are set to ensure that the functions of companies are properly undertaken, that they are able to finance their activities, that interests of customers are protected and that companies are efficient in carrying out their functions.

A stylised description of the way in which this process operates is as follows (Figure 1). Levels and quality of service laid down by legislation or regulation influence the capital base and required capital expenditure of water companies. Together these establish the minimum value of assets on which water companies should be able to earn a reasonable rate of return. Estimates are made of the efficient operating costs at which services can be provided; minimum profits and operating costs then determine revenues and therefore prices.

These principles are complicated by the financial obligations that the large capital expenditures impose on water companies. In setting prices at privatisation, account had to be taken of the debt obligation associated with the financing of capital expenditures as well as their rates of return. Financial ratios rather than rates of return on capital have in practice constrained prices to date.

Regulation has therefore been concerned with establishing quality and service standards, evaluating the levels of capital expenditure that are associated with meeting these standards, determining a rate of return on capital, examining the financial condition of water companies, evaluating efficient levels of operating expenditure and monitoring the implementation of capital expenditures and the provision of services.

Performance

At least three parties are interested in the performance of water companies – customers, investors, and local communities. From the point of view of customers, the key characteristics are quality of service and price. Investors are interested in rates of return on capital

Figure 1: Principles of Price Regulation

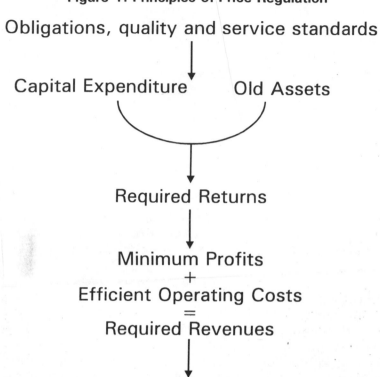

Obligations, quality and service standards

Capital Expenditure   Old Assets

Required Returns

Minimum Profits
+
Efficient Operating Costs
=
Required Revenues

Prices

employed. Communities are concerned about pollution and environmental factors.

There has been significant progress in relation to all three parties. There have been improvements in some but not all aspects of water quality, customer services and sewerage services. On most criteria investors have been well rewarded since privatisation. Rates of return on equity have been high, in excess of stock market returns as a whole and in excess of the cost of capital of the industry. Considerable effort is going into improvement of river quality and bathing water. Discharges into rivers and seas are set to decline appreciably.

The one area in which there has clearly not been an improvement is price. The real price of water and sewerage services has risen appreciably since privatisation. To establish whether these price increases have been justified it is necessary to consider the principles of price

25

regulation. As described above, prices are set on the basis of projections of investment, costs of capital and minimum costs of production. If firms achieve lower costs of production, then they keep the rewards that they have earned. If they are less efficient than predicted they earn less than the cost of capital.

Over any particular regulatory period firms retain any abnormal profits they earn. At the end of a regulatory period prices are determined on the basis of new predictions of efficient costs of production and firms are set the target of beating these new efficiency projections. The important point to note here is that prices are set on an *ex ante* basis; they are not adjusted *ex post* to claw back abnormal profits or losses. If they were firms would be subject to rate of return rather than price regulation and this would significantly blunt their incentives to pursue cost savings.

That water companies have earned returns that are in excess of the cost of capital is indicative of the fact that they were able to attain lower than predicted costs. Provided that this has not come at the expense of quality of services, they have more than attained their goal. It is true that targets may initially have been set generously to facilitate privatisation, but to question now whether lower costs could have been attained is no more valid than a head office of a company berating a division that has more than attained its targets for not doing still better.

The above discussion suggests that the water companies' performance since privatisation has been quite satisfactory. In most cases they have achieved quality standards and done so at a cost that is below that which was predicted at the time of privatisation. Judged by its initial standards, privatisation has been a success.

There are, however, a number of qualifications to this sanguine view.

Problems

Much of the increase in price that has occurred since privatisation is due to the large capital expenditure programmes that the water companies have undertaken. This raises two questions.

o *First*, is this high level of capital expenditure justified? Does it really reflect preferences of customers and communities for improved quality and environment.

o *Second*, even if it is warranted, have standards been delivered at minimum costs?

Market Surveys

An attempt has been made to answer the first through customer surveys. OFWAT asked the 10 water and sewerage companies to perform surveys of customers' willingness to pay for higher standards. The results suggested a range of different views. In some regions, there was a marked reluctance to accept higher prices. In others, quality improvements were felt to be justified.

These surveys are difficult to interpret not only because of their contradictory results but also because of the way in which they were undertaken. The surveys were organised by parties with clear vested interests in their outcomes, namely the water companies. Suppose that one water company believes it is rewarded for new investment at a rate of return which is in excess of its cost of capital. For this company the maximum attainable level of investment is desirable. For another water company that believes new investment is rewarded at less than its cost of capital, minimum investment is desirable. The first company will therefore have an incentive to record a customer preference for significantly improved standards and the second for minimum standards. The familiar problems associated with designing truly objective surveys would lead the cynic to conclude that their results reflect no more than companies' beliefs about the relation of returns to their cost of capital.

Comparative Cost Exercises

Leaving aside this question of whether quality standards reflect consumer preferences and turning to the second question of whether particular standards are delivered at minimum costs, it is necessary to consider first how minimum costs could be judged. There are two components to this: current expenditures and capital costs.

In contrast to its predecessors, the privatisation of the water industry entailed the creation of a number of separate companies. The scope for direct competition between water companies was limited by geographical and natural monopoly considerations. However, yardstick competition was thought to be a surrogate for actual competition. According to yardstick competition, comparisons can be made between the cost structures of different companies and prices set on the basis of minimum or average industry costs as against actual costs of individual companies. There is a view that this mirrors the operation of actual competition between firms in aggregating information on relevant determinants of performance and providing firms with more powerful incentives to improve performance than would be the case in a monopoly market.

The difficulty that has arisen in practice is that the regionalised utilities operate in more heterogeneous markets than is normally assumed for competing firms. There are numerous specific factors that influence the minimum-cost base of firms: density of population, age of infrastructure and endowments of natural resources (rivers, reservoirs) are some examples. In practice, it has therefore proved to be formidably difficult to establish 'relevant' determinants of performance in the water industry. Identification of minimum costs of production is therefore at a less advanced stage than was originally anticipated and it will be little more of a science in this regulatory round than it was at privatisation.

Costs of Capital

Capital costs raise similar efficiency issues. But two further problems arise as well. The first comes from the fact that the returns from an investment accrue over its life and not just at the time at which the expenditure is incurred. As a consequence, there is a question of how returns should be spread over the life of an asset. This is done on the basis of the cost of capital which, together with the depreciation charge, ensures that the present value of earnings is just equal to the initial capital expenditure. Determination of the cost of capital has, however, been a subject of considerable controversy.

The problem that has arisen is that there is no simple way in which the reward for the risk associated with equity investments could be established. The risk premium of equity investments over and above riskless returns cannot be measured directly. The indirect measures that are available from past data are difficult to interpret.

Following the publication of the MMC report on British Gas, costs of capital of utilities looked set to lie in the 6-8 per cent range. OFFER has suggested costs of capital for the transmission business of the Scottish electricity companies at the bottom of the range. Water companies could be argued to be comparatively safe and therefore to have a cost of capital that lies at or below the bottom of the range.

One of the clearest tests of whether these are appropriate measures of the cost of capital comes from looking at share price reactions to the MMC and subsequent announcements by other regulators. The fact that costs of capital will lie in the range of 6-8 per cent does not appear to have caused stock markets much disquiet. If anything, utility share prices have gone up relative to general stock market indices since the MMC announcement.

Asset Valuation

Costs of capital for utilities may therefore be less controversial than seemed likely to be the case until recently. Instead, more attention is now being devoted to the valuation of assets. The value that should be attributed to new capital expenditures is clear-cut: it is simply the expenditures incurred. However, it is less clear how assets that were in place at the time of privatisation should be valued.

A number of suggestions have been made: the current cost value of assets, the current market value of assets, and the value of assets at privatisation updated for price changes and new investments that have occurred since then have all been proposed. Current cost values cannot be employed in the water industry: they are around 10 times the market value of water companies. Current market values suffer from the serious deficiency that they reflect expectations of future regulation. They are therefore a poor basis on which to establish future prices.

The original value of assets at privatisation has the attraction of ensuring that investors are properly rewarded for the assets they origin-ally acquired. If new capital expenditures are added to this, total investments expect to earn the cost of capital at each regulatory review.

There is some discussion about the date at which the initial value of privatisation assets should be measured, how cash injections that were associated with privatisation assets should be treated, and whether advancements associated with financial ratios should be clawed back. However, the principles that should guide these issues are clear-cut.

Capital Efficiency Savings

A more serious difficulty concerns the treatment of efficiency gains. As noted above, the principle of price regulation is that firms should be able to retain efficiency gains achieved between regulatory reviews. At regulatory reviews, prices reflect lower operating costs. However, if these efficiency gains have resulted from investments by companies, then they should be carried forward to future reviews in the form of higher asset values. There is, in other words, an unobservable capital investment and such expenditures are a valid cause of a divergence of market from book value of a company. They are most obviously associated with developing customer relations, corporate restructurings and R&D.

The determination of where efficiency gains have been more than anticipated is formidably difficult. Instead, the appropriate response is to place the burden of proof on companies. It is the water companies which should be able to demonstrate that efficiency savings have been greater than anticipated at the last regulatory review. In the absence of such evidence, only agreed expenditures on capital investments should be capitalised.

In sum, there are a number of details associated with regulation that still require clarification. However, the general operation of the regulatory system is now clear and by the time of the next periodic review it can be expected with a reasonable degree of confidence that the remaining problems highlighted above will have been solved.

Alternatives

The Structure of Regulation

The main problems that will remain are the determination of quality standards and the monitoring of their implementation. Market surveys have not been an adequate basis on which to establish customer preferences. Instead, resort has had to be made to the Secretary of State to clarify the quality/price trade-off. This largely removes regional autonomy from standard setting and allows for little geographical variation.

Market surveys can relate only to a segment of the total capital expenditure programme, namely, that component which is related to discretionary spending. Much of the industry's investments result from statutory obligations emanating from domestic and international legislation. These obligations should have been subject to proper cost-benefit analysis. However, that process has been hindered by the structure of the UK regulatory system which separates the setting of standards from their costing and charging. There are some merits in this separation insofar as in principle separation allows the process of setting and implementing standards to be made more transparent. But this requires that those who are concerned with the setting of standards should be obliged to provide explicit estimates of their costs. Disaggregation of K factors in water and sewerage charges into environmental, quality and efficiency components would make customers better informed about the costs of different programmes and assist in the determination of social preferences.

Domestic regulation is further restricted by European Community law. The merit of harmonisation of regulation of drinking water and sewage disposal across member-nations of the EC is highly question-able. Harmonisation of regulation is justified only where there are:

(a) cross-border externalities;

(b) a unique optimal form of regulation; or

(c) competition issues raised by failure to harmonise (for example, barriers to entry of foreign firms).

Few of these apply to drinking water and the only area where (a) might be relevant is in river quality and discharge of sludge to the sea. Elsewhere, water regulation is a classic example of an industry in which principles of subsidiarity should operate and legislation should be delegated to member-states. Furthermore, quality of water and possibly pollution control beyond minimum standards should be a matter of regional as against national legislation except where there are clear spillovers across regions.

Privatisation versus Franchising

The need for cost comparisons would be diminished if an element of actual as against yardstick competition could be introduced into the provision of water and sewerage services. In practice, 'Inset' agree-ments (by which outside companies can bid to supply particular customers) and franchises of specific operations are not easy to operate. There are serious difficulties of determining appropriate intercon-nection charges for outside operators entering another company's region.

One way in which both problems of regional determination of quality standards and actual as against yardstick competition could have been resolved is through retaining ownership of assets under regional control and creating general water utility companies that competed for fran-chises to operate regional and local operations. This is the approach used in France and close to a system that has been contemplated in Scotland. It has many attractions in comparison with the current system of private ownership of assets which operates in England and Wales.

Franchising suffers from some well-known problems. In particular, there are problems of ensuring a fair basis on which new entrants can compete with incumbents. Furthermore, if assets are retained under public control, capital as against operating efficiency incentives are blunted. Franchising is not therefore a serious option so long as capital expenditures remain at anything like their current level. However, in the longer term, as expenditures diminish and further operating efficiencies are sought, pressures for returning assets to public control will increase.

Problems of eliciting public preferences for quality standards and minimising costs will therefore remain. The water industry is not exceptional in facing a problem of determining public preferences; however, it is clearly correct that the rights of international organisations to dictate standards, in particular those that have not been properly costed, should be questioned. Furthermore, attempts to elicit local as against national preferences should be made, though the water companies themselves are probably not the appropriate medium.

Q Ratios[1]

Cost minimisation is less of a difficulty than it appears. A primary function of a capital market is to encourage companies to maximise productive efficiency. This occurs through pressure on firms to maximise their stock market prices. In the absence of a market for corporate control prior to the elimination of the golden share, this incentive is blunted but it is still present through managerial remuneration schemes and the direct pressure that institutions can bring to bear on companies.

Against this background, establishing whether companies are allowed to charge unduly high prices is relatively straightforward. If charges are too high, the market value of water companies will be high in relation to the value of assets employed. In other words, where regulation is unduly lax the ratio of the market value of companies to their rolled forward market values plus new investment will be in excess of unity.

This provides the regulator with a check on the stance of regulation. At each periodic review a comparison should be made between the market value of water companies and their rolled forward value from the last periodic review. Unduly high charges will be evidenced by market values that are high in relation to rolled forward values. Incentives to capital efficiency savings can be provided by using averages of market to book ratios across the industry as a whole as against actual values of particular companies. Underlying book values of assets adjusted for the discount of market to book values at privatisation therefore provide an appropriate anchor for the market values of assets.

---

[1] Tobin's 'Q' is the ratio of the market value of a company to its current cost book value.

Conclusions

While one can invariably quibble with specific aspects, the operation and regulation of the water industry has by most accounts been a success. A massive capital expenditure programme is in the process of being implemented at the same time as numerous improvements to services are being introduced.

There have been significant problems with the regulation of the financial aspects of the water industry. Determination of costs of capital, asset values and cost comparisons have proved difficult. But these are real problems and there are no easy solutions. What distinguishes the water from other privatised industries is the degree of consultation that has taken place. The industry may at times have felt that consultation has been a one-way process but there clearly has been an attempt to reach some consensus about solutions to these difficult problems.

There is now a fairly clear notion of how regulation will operate in the future. I have attempted to indicate areas in which I expect there may be further developments. The problems that will remain are the determination of standards and the monitoring of their efficient implementation.

CHAIRMAN'S COMMENTS

Ian Byatt
OFWAT

I AGREE WITH A GREAT DEAL in Colin's paper. Regulation has a big political dimension, as well as the economic and financial dimensions that Colin talked about. He mentioned consultation with the industry but, of course, there is also consultation with the public and with politicians. Utilities will never be far away from the public eye and that involves quite a lot of work and activity. Also, a lot of attention needs to be given to the structure of the system, where it was left in a very open and, I think, in some ways, rather unsatisfactory way. Colin mentioned the relationship between the different regulators and the need to link it up in the right ways.

Of course I feel, having listened to Colin, that how could you possibly expect a tiny little office to cope with all those problems and difficulties? This raises an interesting point about the way regulation should work, I believe. One way of approaching it would be to say, it is clear that the small office which Ian Byatt has up in Birmingham cannot cope with all this, especially as each big company has a regulatory team which is probably almost as big as his office. And, there are 30 of them; some are small but many are quite large – some very large – so all the problems are multiplied by 30. One answer would be that the regulator ought to hire enormous staffs to do all these things and the taxpayer should provide him with the necessary resources.

The other way is to recognise that there will be a great deal of art as well as science in this activity. It would be wrong to expect everything to be pinned down in a fully detailed way. I think that it is valuable to have regulation which works by price caps rather than by cost plus. Cost plus is a very gilt-edged way of doing things. It should be gilt-edged in both directions, both in terms of how things are specified and how things are rewarded. I do not think that is the way we should do it. It is right that regulation should be forward-looking in the way in which

Colin suggested. He made some very valuable points about the difficulty of 'defining the functions of a water company'. The regulator is there to ensure that water companies carry out their functions and can finance them. But the law does not offer too much guidance about exactly what those functions are. And in one area, the quality aspect, I did find it necessary to go to the Secretary of State to ask for some clarification. Very large sums of money are at stake. There are many other areas where pinning down the functions in fine detail would not be a very profitable way of doing things.

In the water industry it is very necessary for the regulator to maintain some kind of restraint on investment. Perhaps those are the wrong words, but I think that investment cannot be completely open-ended. Colin puts it in terms of a burden of proof, that companies have to prove that they need to spend certain sums of money. That is probably a good way of putting it.

Two further points. On the question of surveys of customers: these are, of course, pretty imperfect things. People have been doing them in other areas as well. They never get absolutely clear-cut answers. I still believe they are worth doing; the process itself is very worthwhile. It was highly desirable that as a method of communicating with their customers, the water companies should ask them what they wanted. That is not the way the public sector works. It works like the old District Commissioner, who knows what it is the natives want and gets on to do the best for them. Late-20th-century life should not be run that way, and I am delighted the water companies did take the initiative. That they did so is more important than precisely what the motives might have been; and the answers have to be looked at very carefully.

The cost of capital is an interesting area about which we can doubtless talk at length. Colin put the water industry in a 6-8 per cent band. But I refuse to be corralled in that way, as he indicated. And I think other regulators have also wanted to get outside that band. Not only do I see real interest rates falling all the time, but also I am fascinated by Olivier Blanchard's view that the equity premium is now between 2 and 3 per cent. I suppose that is a worldwide number. If we are in a worldwide capital market, that may be the way we should go.

3

REGULATING AIRPORTS
AND AIRLINES

David Starkie[*]
Putnam, Hayes & Bartlett Ltd

The Regulatory Framework

THE STRUCTURE OF REGULATION governing UK airports is still relatively new, dating from the Airports Act 1986. This was primarily concerned with the privatisation of the British Airports Authority, but it also sets out the basic regulatory framework surrounding all UK airports of any significant size. It confers wide-ranging powers on the Secretary of State for Transport, covering matters such as the transfer of local authority airport undertakings to the private sector, the allocation of traffic between airports serving the same area, and the control of air traffic movements at congested airports. However, as with the other major utilities, the main regulatory rôle falls to a special regulator – the Civil Aviation Authority (CAA).

The CAA already existed at the time the Airports Act was passed, and had built up considerable experience in regulating air transport as well as airport safety. In addition, it was, and continues to be, a provider of air traffic control services. From the outset, therefore, it was a rather different animal from other utility regulators such as OFTEL and OFGAS. And while its powers under the Airports Act are broadly comparable with those of other regulators in their own spheres, there are some important differences. In particular, the CAA has no statutory duty to promote competition. Rather, it is charged with furthering the reasonable interests of airport users, promoting efficient,

* David Starkie is particularly grateful to his colleague, Simon Ellis, for assistance in preparing this paper. The views expressed are solely those of the author.

economic and profitable operation and encouraging investment. I shall return to this issue later. Here I simply note that this signifies a different view of the potential for competition from that taken in the case of other privatisations.

Discussion of the CAA's rôle in airport regulation usually focusses on the price formulae applied to a number of our major airports, but in practice its remit goes rather wider. Any UK airport with a turnover in excess of £1 million in at least two of the last three financial years is subject to economic regulation. This means that it must seek permission from the CAA to levy charges and abide by any conditions which the CAA imposes in granting permission. According to the most recent CAA Annual Report, some 32 airports are now subject to economic regulation. There cannot be many businesses of a comparable size which must seek permission from a regulatory body to charge for their services, and I note that the CAA is now arguing for an increase in the turnover threshold.

'Designated' Airports – More Stringent Regulation

Of course, not all airports are subject to the same level of regulation. More stringent regulation is reserved for airports 'designated' by the Secretary of State for Transport under section 40 of the Airports Act. At present there are four such airports – Heathrow, Gatwick, Stansted and Manchester – but in principle the list could be extended. In addition to disclosing certain accounting information, including information on subsidies received, these airports must also restrict the level of traffic charges in accordance with maxima set down by the CAA. Charges are reviewed every five years, at which time restrictions can be modified.

The method by which charges are actually regulated – the application of an RPI-X formula – has, of course, been adopted in a number of privatisations and it is now part of regulatory folklore. But again, there are some important differences in the airports case. It is, so far as I am aware, the only case in which RPI-X style regulation has been applied to an enterprise still in public ownership – that is, Manchester airport (although the Government's intention is that Manchester too should be privatised). In addition, the airports case is unique in terms of the way the formula has been applied. It limits airport charges at the three London airports *collectively*, as well as applying to Heathrow and Gatwick *individually*. And while it limits only certain charges, namely those related to landing, taking off and parking aircraft and handling passengers through terminals, the CAA is required to take into account the airport's total revenue when setting the value of X. This so-called 'single-till' principle looks particularly odd when it is remembered that regulated charges account for perhaps two-fifths of the London airports' revenue.

As the Chairman of the CAA argued in his LBS lecture last year, these anomalies mean that airport regulation is particularly complex. Moreover, under the Act it is the MMC – a non-specialist body – which undertakes the initial stage of the quinquennial review of charges at designated airports. In advising the CAA, the MMC must take account of all the airport's activities, the need to encourage investment and, in the London case, the relationship between three separate airports. In addition, it can make separate public interest findings which the CAA must implement, as it did earlier this year in respect of the provision of certain cost information to users of Manchester airport. Clearly, all this represents an onerous task for a body which cannot claim any specialist knowledge of the industry.

Regulation of Airlines

By contrast, the regulation of airlines is now relatively straightforward, at least in respect of intra-EC routes. Safety regulation continues much as it always has, but following the adoption of the Third Stage Package of European Council Regulations, the economic regulation applying to EC routes is arguably the most liberal in the world. From the beginning of this year, airlines established in the EC and owned and controlled by EC nationals, require only a single Operating Licence, granted by a competent national authority, to fly on most domestic and European routes. Full access to member-states' domestic markets will be permitted by 1997. In addition, the distinction between scheduled and charter flights has been removed, and EC airlines are now free to charge whatever fares they wish on intra-EC flights without any need for prior approval (although there are regulatory safeguards regarding excessively high fares and fares which are predatory).

The CAA has been designated as the competent authority for granting Operating Licences in the UK. As with airport regulation, it has no statutory duty to promote competition. However, under the Civil Aviation Act 1982, it is charged with encouraging UK airlines to provide a range of services and with furthering the reasonable interests of airline users. And it is clear from various policy statements that the

CAA regards competition within the framework of a multi-airline industry as the best way of achieving these objectives.[1]

Against this background, the CAA can be expected to adopt a liberal stance in administering the new régime wherever it has discretion. For example, on the question of financial monitoring, its stated policy is to minimise intervention in order to concentrate on airlines whose financial failure would have the most impact. It has also introduced a separate Operating Licence for small-scale operators in order to minimise the regulatory burden on air taxis; before the new EC regulations came into force these services were exempt from licensing in the UK.

Of course, we are still a long way from 'open skies' the world over. In order to fly to destinations outside the EC, airlines also require separate Route Licences and route access is still largely determined by bilateral negotiations between governments. However, the Third EC Package is still a major step on the way to a more open and competitive airline industry.

Having outlined the regulatory framework for civil aviation, I now want to examine the efficiency and effectiveness of this framework and to suggest areas in which the framework might be modified and refocussed.

Airports: Regulatory Weaknesses

Here I believe there are inconsistencies or weaknesses in the framework and the way it is implemented. I have already noted that the CAA has no statutory duty to promote competition between airports, and this perhaps reflects a rather pessimistic view of the prospects for competition. But such a view sits rather awkwardly with S.41(3)(c) of the Airports Act. This section gives the CAA the power to impose conditions when it is judged that an airport operator has fixed charges which are insufficient to cover the costs of a service or facility and those charges materially harm the business of another airport operator; in other words, the section is aimed at predatory pricing. But for there to be a possibility of predatory pricing, there has to be a prospect for competition and yet, as noted, the Act does not embrace this prospect.

This tension in the legislation arguably reflects the different points of view forcefully promoted in the mid-1980s. The local authority airports, led by Manchester, were fearful that subsidised development

---

[1] The Secretary of State for Transport's objectives for the airline industry, from the 1984 White Paper, *Airline Competition Policy* (Cmnd.9366), include promoting competition in all markets.

at Stansted might affect their future prospects and wanted to level the playing field by splitting the ownership of British Airports Authority. The Authority, naturally, opposed any such move.[2]

Revisiting the 1985 Airports Policy White Paper to see how the Government balanced these different opinions makes for interesting reading. The Government did not dismiss out of hand the notion that competition between airports was possible but concluded that the opportunities were limited and especially so where Heathrow was concerned. On the other hand, dividing the ownership of the Authority's airports would have undermined an important plank of policy, namely, the Traffic Distribution Rules. At the time it was considered that the problem of capacity shortfalls at existing South-Eastern airports could be tackled by directing traffic between airports; distribution rules were first introduced at Heathrow in 1977. It was envisaged that further intervention would be necessary and by having an integrated airport system under common ownership, this would both facilitate the administration of such a policy and minimise its commercial impact.

The Government concluded, therefore, that the option of selling the Authority's airports individually was unlikely to bring substantial real advantages, and to have some important disadvantages. But to address the cross-subsidy issue it went for a transparent accounting structure and S41(3)(c). The White Paper commented: 'The Government believes that these arrangements taken together will ensure that demand is not attracted away from the regions by price-cutting in the South East', a comment, incidentally, which seems to cut across its view that the opportunities for price competition were limited.

Market Influence Permitted in Traffic Distribution

Since 1985, however, aviation policy has changed in one important respect, namely, a substantial modification of the Traffic Distribution Rules. Since 1991 all airlines have been free to operate scheduled services from Heathrow and whole-plane charters are no longer barred (subject, of course, to the necessary route authorisations and access to scarce runway slots). What we see here is a loosening of the regulatory structure and an increasing willingness to let the market influence the allocation of airline traffics.

---

[2] For an early discussion of this issue, see David Starkie and David Thompson, *Privatising London's Airports*, Institute of Fiscal Studies, Report 16, 1985; and David Starkie and David Thompson, 'Stansted: A Viable Investment?', *Fiscal Studies*, Vol.7, No.3, 1986, pp.76-81.

Interestingly, S41(3)(c) is now being put to the test – for the first time.[3] London Luton Airport has lodged a complaint with the CAA alleging that BAA is abusing its monopoly position and behaving anti-competitively by cross-subsidising operations at Stansted. The complaint was lodged in June 1993 and a response is expected shortly. It would be invidious of me to comment on the merits of this particular case. But I wish to make some general observations about the wording of the legislation and the complainant's task.

The complainant is required to show to the satisfaction of the CAA that charges relating to 'relevant activities' (which are defined as services or facilities for the purpose of landing, parking, taking-off and servicing of aircraft and for the purposes of handling passengers and cargo):

o are insufficient to cover costs; *or*

o are artificially low; *and*

o materially harm; *or*

o are intended to materially harm other airport businesses.

Therefore, it is not necessary to show that the low charges were *intended* to harm, only that such harm has occurred. Nor is it necessary to show that the charges are insufficient in relation to costs; it will suffice to show that charges are 'artificially low'. This is defined in Section 41(4) as a charge which is significantly lower than it otherwise would have been because of a subsidy or because, where the airport is a company, it has failed *inter alia* to achieve a reasonable return on capital employed.

Thus, the case can be argued on alternate grounds and, for example, to argue that charges are artificially low might be considered an easier task than arguing revenues are insufficient to cover costs once the complexities of allocating costs and deciding upon an appropriate measure for them are borne in mind. Similarly, to show that material harm has taken place might be easier than to show intent to harm. And the introduction of a requirement to achieve a reasonable return on past

---

[3] Section 41 of the Act has been used on a previous occasion; a number of airlines jointly and successfully brought a complaint under Section 41(2), arguing that Heathrow Airport Limited adopted a pricing policy which unreasonably discriminated between users.

investment adds an interesting perspective. An economist might wish to argue that efficient charges should disregard sunk costs; the wording of the legislation would appear to preclude this possibility.

Application of European Competition Law

As for the application of European competition law to this matter there is, as yet, no specific directive on airport charges to provide a framework. Nevertheless, Articles 85 and 86 provide a means for bringing a complaint of unfair competition and, in the current context, provide a possible alternative to seeking remedies under Section 41 of the 1986 Airports Act (the complainant will, of course, need to demonstrate that trade between member-states has been affected). An Article 86 case has the feature that transgressors can be heavily penalised and therefore the *threat* alone of an investigation may make companies think again about their conduct. In contrast, a Section 41 case can lead only to the application of conditions regulating future conduct. In addition, an Article 86 case will consider a narrower range of issues than a complaint brought under Section 41. Under a Section 41 case the CAA must be satisfied that the airport operator is not only pursuing a course of conduct specified in the Act but the authority must also consider that the conduct is appropriate to the remedy.[4]

Whilst there are differences of opinion on the degree to which competition between airports is feasible, there is, nevertheless, general agreement that airports can possess market power and in the case of large airports – Heathrow is a prime example – this market power may be substantial. It is for this reason that Section 40 of the Airports Act allows the Secretary of State to designate particular airports and to subject their charges for landings, aircraft parking and passenger handling to a price cap. As I have already noted, four airports are currently designated – Heathrow, Gatwick, Stansted and Manchester.

Airport Designation Criteria: Stansted and the Scottish Airports

As one might expect, there has been no pronouncement on the criteria that are applied in the designation process but I am sure that the designation of Heathrow, Gatwick and Manchester meets with general approval. Stansted is a more curious case; it is relatively small in terms

---

[4] Since the paper was delivered, the CAA has announced its decision on Luton's complaint. The Authority found that the Section 41(3)(c) tests were met but did not consider that Stansted's conduct was appropriate to remedy. London Luton Airport are proposing to take their complaint to the European Commission.

of traffic volume and is trying hard to attract traffic; it is not clear why at this stage of its development it should have been designated. Indeed, it is not subject to a limitation on its charges as such but, because the price cap applies collectively to all three London airports, an increase in charges at Stansted implies a decrease at Heathrow and Gatwick. You may consider this to be a rather perverse outcome (although its practical effect is still very small).

It is almost eight years since the four airports were designated and the interesting question is whether and when the list might be extended. In the mid-1980s, Manchester handled around 6 million terminal passengers but most of these were on charter flights; charter flights could be considered relatively footloose in terms of airport used (because leisure passengers are generally more willing to use an alternative) and, arguably, the real market power of airports applies in relation to scheduled traffic. It is interesting to note that scheduled traffic in 1992 was also in the range 2-3 million at Birmingham, Edinburgh and Glasgow airports. Of course, if there is no evidence of overcharging at such airports nor of inefficiencies in their operation, there is nothing to be gained by designation; it would then become merely regulation for its own sake, and one of the advantages of not having rigid criteria is that one can be flexible in the approach adopted.

Nevertheless, there is some indication that charges at the airports operated by BAA's subsidiary, Scottish Airports Ltd, are higher than they need be. Scottish Airports Ltd has a dominant position in its regional market; it owns the three largest airports in Scotland (Glasgow, Edinburgh and Aberdeen), and accounts for about 90 per cent of Scottish traffics. Early this year, the Scottish Affairs Committee of the House of Commons considered the question: Has BAA used its dominant position to levy unreasonably high landing charges at its Scottish airports? It examined average revenue yields per passenger and found these to be high relative to the (controlled) yields at the London airports. It also referred to MMC evidence which suggested that rates of return on capital employed at Glasgow and Edinburgh exceeded comparable figures at Gatwick. The Committee, therefore, suggested that both Glasgow and Edinburgh be designated and their charges subject to regulation.

On the face of it, it does seem surprising that BAA's Scottish airports were not at the time designated along with Manchester and the London airports. The reason was that the group as a whole was barely profitable (although terminal capacity was generally well used) and there was the hopeless commercial case of Prestwick. Prestwick was propped up for political reasons and was the designated gateway for long-haul Scottish routes (as a consequence of which there were no regular long-haul scheduled services(!)). Price capping would have reduced the scope for cross-subsidy and undermined government policy for Scotland's airports. Of course, Prestwick is no longer the gateway airport for Scotland and it is no longer owned by BAA.

The Single-Till Principle – Another Anomaly

During last year's lecture,[5] the Chairman of the CAA drew attention to another anomaly (that is my term, not his) in the regulatory structure, namely, the single-till principle. The charges that are regulated are those only for certain airside activities; the so-called commercial activities (duty-free sales, other terminal retailing, car parking, etc.) are not price-capped, they account for most revenues, and their revenue stream is taken into account when judging an appropriate value for X in the RPI-X formula. Thus, for any given revenue requirement, an increase in the proportion of revenues from unregulated activities requires an offsetting adjustment from the regulated activities through a (relatively large) change in the value for X. As Christopher Chataway pointed out, in the extreme this may lead to negative charges for runway and terminal use. Now, in certain circumstances, where capacity can be added only in large amounts and this leads initially to low utilisation, the effects of the one-till approach are not altogether adverse in terms of economic efficiency. But where capacity is well used and where it cannot be easily adjusted, the combination of an RPI-X formula and a single-till philosophy can lead to ludicrous results – the pressure is to reduce charges in spite of growing airside congestion. This is precisely the situation with respect to runway charges at Heathrow and Gatwick.

This makes it more difficult to manage the limited capacity available, it re-inforces the incumbents' so-called 'grandfather rights' to landing slots, and it has the effect of passing the rents associated with airports of superior location to the airlines, most of which are established outside the UK and the EC. As Christopher Chataway remarked, the intrinsic logic of the single-till principle will need to be reconsidered

---

[5] See Rt. Hon. Christopher Chataway, 'Airports and Airline Competition', in M.E. Beesley (ed.), *Major Issues in Regulation*, IEA Readings No. 40, London: Institute of Economic Affairs in association with the London Business School, 1993, pp. 141-51, at pp. 148-49.

and it is possible that the recent developments in the Heathrow arbitration case – the Award and the Counter Claim – might provide an opportunity for a start to be made.

Airlines: The 'Third Package'

Turning now to airline matters, the major issue here is how well the 'third package' is working, what is to be expected from it, and whether the regulatory safeguards are appropriate. The regulatory safeguards concern mergers and acquisitions, the control of anti-competitive behaviour and monopoly pricing. I shall concentrate on the latter issues.

The view promoted by the popular press is that liberalisation in European aviation can be expected to lead to an era of cheap fares. Frequent reference is made to developments in the USA where, following deregulation, domestic fares tumbled not only in nominal but also in real terms as competitors flooded into the market. Of course, in recent years the US industry has seen a spate of mergers, acquisitions and insolvency, so that the levels of concentration in the industry are not all that different today than they were in, say, 1979. In spite of this, for both quality and price of the product, there remain significant differences from the regulated era. The picture is a complex one and prevents easy generalisation but real fares on the whole are well down on previous levels (although it must be remembered that at current levels of fares, collectively, US airlines are making losses). If comparisons are to be drawn I would suggest that it is this 'matured' stage of the US industry that forms a more realistic benchmark.

Against this benchmark one can note significant differences in the European environment: a much more constrained airport and airspace infrastructure; generally less dense and shorter routes; a culture of bilateralism, capacity sharing and revenue pooling; and an industry cost base which is high by US standards (although some of the inflated costs reflect the different operating environment). This suggests that perhaps we should not expect too much too quickly. It will take time for inefficient costs to be shaken-out (even where there is a will to do so), and in the short term the infrastructure constraints can only be eased. Therefore, I think it unrealistic to expect perfectly competitive behaviour (with notions of an equality between fares and marginal costs), especially where it is often the case that markets are thin, or where capacity is exogenously determined and limited by runway and airspace constraints.

Lessons of US Experience Since Deregulation

What, therefore, can we expect? Here again, I think it is useful to turn to US experience. During the 1980s, there was a concentration of effort by US academics and others towards examining whether the airline industry was contestable – the idea that in the absence of sunk costs the possibility of hit-and-run entry produces perfectly competitive behaviour even in markets with few players. The industry was found not to conform to the contestability ideal; the number of airlines flying a route (the degree of concentration) did affect fare levels. More recently, analysts have turned their attention to examining competitive *conduct* on concentrated routes in order to explain pricing behaviour.

This is producing a rich vein of information, especially for duopoly routes which are characteristic of European aviation. What the studies have shown is that in the deregulated US market where two airlines fly a route, the outcome as a rule is not perfectly competitive behaviour but neither is behaviour fully collusive; the tendency is for the airlines to be competitive to a degree. Put another way, we can say that on duopoly routes price competition is moderate rather than vigorous and that, importantly, collusion on price is absent. Other inferences can be drawn from this material. These include: the carrier with a higher share of a duopoly route market tends to price more competitively; carriers price more competitively on longer-distance routes and on routes that are predominantly leisure oriented; and, of course, the more competing carriers the more price competitive the route becomes.

Expectations in Europe

I believe that this type of information provides a useful point of reference when turning to expectations in Europe. It provides a guide for the regulator and it suggests that the regulator should focus on whether behaviour in the market is appropriately non-co-operative. The initial aim should be to undermine the culture that has traditionally prevailed in the European market and to get flag-carrying airlines competing in their duopoly markets. In this context I am reasonably optimistic that this can be achieved for reasons I shall now explain.

A recent analysis of the route structure of Western European schedule aviation by Richard Pryke of Liverpool University[6] has shown that, compared with the United States, European routes (including those in

---

[6] Richard Pryke, 'American Deregulation and European Liberalisation', in David Banister and Kenneth Button (eds.), *Transport in a Free Market Economy*, London: Macmillan, 1991.

the European Economic Area countries) are less monopolistic where there are few flights. For example, half the European routes with 20-29 one-way flights per week have two or more carriers, whereas the corresponding proportion for the USA is only a sixth. This difference is explained by bilateral agreements which lead to both national carriers flying on international routes. But it does mean that, in effect, Europe has a potentially more competitive network structure; often thin routes are served by more than one airline. It probably also means that on a number of thin routes there are more seats offered than might be warranted by market demand. Couple this with the possibility that, in terms of productive efficiency, European airlines are currently *di*verging (with some but not all national carriers seriously seeking efficiencies), and one can see that there is a strong incentive for particular airlines to cast aside the traditions of co-operation and to seek advantage from a more competitive strategy.

This is merely an hypothesis and, of course, one can start from a different set of assumptions – that liberalisation will lead to more monopolies in thin markets (this was Pryke's working assumption) or that mergers and acquisitions will have the same effect. Much will depend upon how the regulator interprets his or her rôle and reads the signals correctly. On the latter there is perhaps some cause for concern.

The Commission is in the process of putting in place safeguards against excessively high tariffs for on-demand fares unencumbered by restrictions on use. Unfortunately, the process appears to be developing a rather mechanistic approach. The principal instrument of analysis is the operating ratio defined as the relationship between total net receipts for a route and the costs incurred on the route. The Commission is inclined to presume an abuse of a dominant position when the operating ratio is exceeded by a specified amount. In addition, even if the overall ratio remains within acceptable limits the Commission may still judge that abuse exists if a 'basic fare' (the lowest fully flexible fare) is considered to be excessively high. To determine whether this is the case the Commission will compare this particular fare with all the direct and indirect costs attributable to the service while taking into account the return on capital as well as factors such as 'acceptable cross-subsidisation between routes'.

Personally, I am uneasy with this type of approach. The cost and revenue allocation problems are considerable, apart from which the process seems to contradict the intent of the liberalisation programme. It also appears to run counter to the dynamics of the competitive process; several studies have shown that in response to greater competition, an airline will actually increase the dispersion of its prices.

Moreover, it does raise a more fundamental issue. If airport capacity is constrained, as it is at many of Europe's principal airports, and it is not the practice for airports to charge market-clearing prices, is it not legitimate therefore for an airline to adopt price rationing? In these circumstances, fares may exceed direct and indirect costs by a substantial amount but the ensuing scarcity rents are not monopoly rents. In the face of these difficulties, it would seem preferable to focus *not* upon the level of fares or their variance, but upon the basic conduct of airlines operating various routes – more along the lines of the US analyses I referred to earlier.

Concluding Remarks: Regulatory Reform

I conclude with a few remarks about the current debate over regulatory reform, and how it relates to aviation. Several commentators have expressed deep disquiet about economic regulation in the UK. It has been variously described as lacking in transparency, unnecessarily antagonistic and too discretionary. Some have argued for greater control of the regulators, through measures such as procedural safeguards governing regulatory decisions and greater accountability. Others have suggested a streamlining of the overall regulatory framework, for example by combining the functions of different regulatory bodies under one roof. The logical extreme of this kind of reform would be a 'super-OFT', with one Director General responsible for the whole panoply of economic regulation.

I certainly share some of these concerns, although I am somewhat more optimistic than many about the basic structure of regulation in the UK. It is true that it often gives a good deal of discretion to individual regulators. This means that they must be men and women of unusual ability, combining a knowledge of economics, business and accountancy with political and diplomatic skills – although some inevitably attach more importance to some of these qualities than others! It is also true that this level of discretion means that individual decisions will be strongly influenced by the personality of the regulator concerned, but I do not see any real difficulty with this. It is not clear to me that the decisions which would emerge from a more constrained and legalistic process would be any better.

Of course, greater discretion for the regulators does mean that their decisions appear inconsistent at times. OFGAS has pushed hard for a break-up of British Gas, but the CAA has fought shy of suggesting a break-up of BAA. This may be partly due to their different objectives – as I noted earlier, the CAA has no duty to promote competition between airports. However, I cannot help wondering that things might have been different if Sir James McKinnon had been appointed Chairman of the CAA! At the same time, while these differences of approach are often understandably frustrating to those who are on the end of the regulators' decisions, they do have a plus side. They allow us to compare and contrast different regulatory experience, in much the same way as some regulators can compare the performance of different firms under yardstick competition, and we can draw valuable lessons from this experience.

Indeed, a good deal more open debate between regulators over issues of common concern, and between regulators and government departments, would be a healthy thing. I sometimes get the impression that, within government in particular, there is a tendency to believe that open disagreement between regulator and Minister is likely to be damaging. But this need not always be the case. Specialist regulators are perhaps better placed than most to question government policy as it affects their particular industry. I am encouraged by the fact that the CAA saw fit to criticise the Government's decision not to refer BA's acquisition of Dan Air to the MMC. More of this kind of open comment would help to test other aspects of aviation policy.

Of course, too much disagreement between different regulatory authorities, especially when it is behind closed doors, can be harmful. When the disagreement becomes apparent, as it inevitably does, it creates uncertainty and makes it difficult for those operating in the regulated market to plan. The apparent disagreement between the DTI and OFGAS over the future structure of British Gas is a case in point.[7] It is perhaps not so much the fact of the disagreement itself that has generated speculation, but the fact that it has only been hinted at in the MMC report and elsewhere. I recognise that the regulators cannot air their views whilst an MMC investigation is underway, but once it has reported they should move quickly and in concert to effect the necessary regulatory changes.

Argument for Regulatory Streamlining Unconvincing

This brings me to the argument for streamlining regulation. I have to say I do not find this very convincing. Where the utilities are

---

[7] 'Making the Break? Regulatory Games and the Future of British Gas', *PHB Insights: 1993*, London: Putnam, Hayes and Bartlett, 1993.

concerned, there are advantages in having specialist regulators, with clear responsibilities in relation to a particular industry. The knowledge and experience they develop are of considerable value when making decisions which will have a fundamental impact on those they are regulating. If regulatory bodies were businesses, this kind of knowledge would constitute a strategic asset. In my view, its value would only be reduced by merger and rationalisation. One regulator cannot hope to gain sufficient command of the issues arising in a whole range of industries. With all due respect to Sir Bryan Carsberg, I think even his abilities would be seriously taxed if he were required to combine his existing duties with his former ones covering telecoms and others covering gas, electricity, water and aviation.

A thorough knowledge of the industry is clearly important. But it is equally important that this expertise is fed into the regulatory process at the right stage. In this context, the relationship between the MMC and the CAA in airport regulation, which I mentioned earlier, looks rather odd. I do not doubt the depth of the MMC's analysis when looking at the question of airport charges, but I think it is better placed to weigh up expert evidence from different parties, rather than provide expert advice to the experts, as at present. It is not entirely clear why the model adopted in the case of telecoms, gas and electricity – negotiation of amendments to licence conditions between the industry and specialist regulator, followed by reference to the MMC if they fail to reach agreement – was not followed in the case of airports. Reading between the lines of the MMC reports on airport charging produced so far, the MMC itself appears to be uneasy with its rôle. It may be time to look again at the procedure and ask whether airports really do merit a different approach.

Overall, however, it seems to me that the broad structure of regulation works reasonably well. The system adopted in the UK, including that applying to airports, has many desirable features – the regulators are experts, they are distanced from the politicians, and their basic powers and responsibilities are clearly set out in law. We would do well to remember this before embarking on a path of wholesale change.

CHAIRMAN'S COMMENTS

Rt Hon Christopher Chataway

Civil Aviation Authority

I WILL START WITH AIRPORTS: David Starkie is absolutely right that a very large number of airports are caught 'within the net'. Though we would like, as he mentioned, to see the threshold raised, so that there are fewer than 30-odd brought within the net, one should not overstate its importance. They are subject to minimum requirements; for example, they have to submit accounts. The grant of permission is more or less automatic. It does not bring any particular consequences.

David has drawn particular attention to a case that we have at the moment, the complaint from Luton Airport about Stansted's pricing policy. I take issue slightly with an argument he deployed. The Act does not actually talk about predatory pricing and it is not predatory pricing, therefore, that any complainant necessarily has to prove. I believe that the Act deliberately avoided that concept, because it can cause great damage inadvertently. If an airport were to cause very considerable damage to another that was to an extent its competitor by its pricing policy, then the Authority can already take action. It is not necessary for the complainant to prove that the prices were lowered with a view to eliminating competition.

The way in which the Act works is that the Authority has the power to require a remedy, but it is not itself required to do so. So, to dictate a remedy, the CAA must find a course of conduct as specified in the Act. We have to find that a remedy is appropriate and necessary, following Section 41, paragraph 2 of the Act. It is therefore impossible for the Authority to find an airport acting as the Act describes, but to refuse to intervene if it does find a remedy that is appropriate and necessary. I must make it absolutely clear that I am not commenting in any way on the rights or wrongs of that particular case.

Single-Till Principle

Can I move now to a quite large issue, the single-till principle? As David Starkie recognised, this is required by treaty; we are not at liberty to decide that we would like to regulate on some other basis and to abandon it. I must say that there does not appear to be any immediate prospect, or early prospect, of any international move to abandon it. And I do not think that recent arbitration, and the disputes that have followed it, are likely to lead to its abandonment.

But it does, as he says, raise increasingly difficult issues. It may be some time, perhaps some very long time, before there is any prospect of the single-till principle leading to a negative charge for landing charges at Heathrow. It might be a little bit sooner, though not really early, at Manchester Airport. But it is always possible, in theory, under the Airports Act to regulate the other charges that go to make up an airport's revenues. It would, in theory, be possible for the regulators at the MMC and the CAA to take the view that there was a position of market dominance, and, therefore, that there should be some limitation, for example, upon car park charges or the property charges. But the more one thinks of that solution, the less attractive it becomes.

It would be bizarre, indeed, if a desire to limit the overall profitability and price levels of an airport operator were to produce parking charges which actually attracted people to park at Heathrow, for example, even though they were not going to use the airport. Even worse, some mechanism might be found for actually passing on the control over prices to the customer. Then people might be attracted to shop at Heathrow even though they had no intention of using the airlines. So that in the longer term there may well be an unresolved conflict between the requirement in the Act to regulate prices and the single-till principle.

CAA and MMC Responsibilities

So far as the division of responsibilities between the CAA and the MMC is concerned, I think that the underlying logic is pretty clear. The reason why the CAA is given the responsibilities it has is that the MMC has experience on trading and concessions, and so on, in which the CAA has no expertise. It is, therefore, reasonable to follow the procedure laid down in the Act whereby the MMC comes first to its view on the non-aviation matters and the CAA, at stage two, looks at the airside charges. I think that the procedure has, in practice, worked well.

Though I do see a reasonable degree of logic in the present operating arrangement between the CAA and the MMC, I do not think that the order in which we bat has necessarily to be fixed. If, over the rest of the regulatory landscape, the practice is to give the MMC the last word, I can think of ways in which that could be organised for airports too.

US and European Experience on Duopoly Routes

I think David made some interesting comparisons between the United States and Europe on airline competition. One is not surprised that on routes that are duopolies there is a bit more competition in the United States than in such routes in Europe. After all, the history of the experience is totally different. In the United States collusion has been discouraged for the last 20 years or so; in Europe, it has been institutionalised and up until fairly recently positively encouraged by governments. So it is not surprising that there are many more duopoly routes in Europe. They are, as David has said, a product of bilateral agreements. Nor is it surprising that in Europe there is now very little competition along those duopoly routes. It is very noticeable that, since the advent of the third package, there is virtually no case of price competition between flag carriers on duopoly routes. The significant examples of price competition this year have come on routes where British Midland is a third carrier.

I think I would be less optimistic than David Starkie is about the prospect of competition between two flag carriers developing on many of those duopoly routes. As he says, a lot will depend upon external factors and much will depend, obviously, upon the seriousness with which the European Commission combats state aid. Even though there may be disparities in efficiency, there is not much incentive for anybody to spend money competing seriously on a duopoly route if he knows that there is a state government behind his competitor who will enable it to maintain market share, however inefficient it might be.

The best prospect of competition is on the major European routes, of which at the moment there is very little sign. I would see the best prospects from the advent of third carriers. All those third carriers need not necessarily be new airlines or non-flag carriers. One very interesting development this year has been the appearance of associate and, potentially, lower-cost subsidiaries of flag carriers. Third airline competition may come from them.

Regulatory Concentration

Finally, I turn to the interesting set of issues which the paper raised about the regulatory framework in the country as a whole. I agree there is little attraction in concentrating regulators into one organisation or even into fewer groupings. Dr Veljanovski has suggested various groupings. One of them was a communications regulator, to include broadcasting as well as aviation. There, the span of expertise that would be required of the regulator might be difficult to assemble.

In the longer term, I can certainly see arguments for there being greater uniformity across the field. David Starkie is absolutely right that there are differences in practice. I may well be wrong but I do not actually think that, if the gas regulator were sitting in my chair, he would want to break up BAA. There are some really quite strong arguments in favour of the proposition that it would be very, very difficult for Stansted (which on its own would, I would be bound to say, probably be bust now), or for Gatwick, effectively to compete against Heathrow.

It does seem to me that there is much to be said for an open discussion on the success or failure of initiatives that have been developed by some of the regulators. Although a number of people have suggested that there should be a much more regular appeal from all regulators' decisions, I do not see, as yet, any very compelling suggestions for better appeal procedures. What you have to avoid, surely, is the situation where there is an almost automatic appeal to the MMC or whomever. This would result in virtually all the major decisions being taken by the one super regulator.

One last thought on the overall regulatory structure: it does seem to me there is something to be said for a corporate organisation. David Starkie said that the individual is likely to influence the outcome. People are inevitably going to matter. It does seem to me unnecessary that the disputes are personalised to the degree that is the case in the present set-up. Something is to be said, therefore, for corporate structures such as the CAA or the MMC. But, overall, it seems to me that the overriding need is for greater transparency. It is that to which, I think, those interested in these issues should be principally addressing themselves.

4

INTERCONNECTION, SEPARATE ACCOUNTING AND THE DEVELOPMENT OF COMPETITION IN UK TELECOMMUNICATIONS

Professor Martin Cave
Brunel University

Introduction

THE AUTUMN OF 1993 is likely to be regarded in the future as a crucial period for the development of competition in UK telecommunications. OFTEL was scheduled to publish its determination of interconnection charges between BT and Mercury and to indicate how it proposed to deal with the access deficit contribution (ADC) waivers. The Director-General of Telecommunications convened a number of workshops on his proposals for interconnection pricing and separate accounting, and stated his intention to make known his decisions on the issues in early 1994.

But in the long term, even these important regulatory decisions are likely to be overwhelmed by more significant developments taking place in the market-place itself. Since mid-1993, there has been an outpouring of new prices for new or existing mobile services, and price cuts by BT. This has been accompanied by further announcements of plans to construct wire-based networks. A further potentially crucial development is the stated intention by BT to push ahead with its plans to offer video-on-demand down the standard copper telephone wire, using digital compression techniques. Although the legal status of this proposal may be challenged (despite the ITC's acknowledgement that it does not require a local delivery licence under broadcasting regulation), it is likely to overturn many of the current assumptions made about

BT's exclusion from the provision of entertainment until 1998 at the earliest, and prompt a re-evaluation of plans by the cable industry.

In this paper I intend to review some of these developments, focussing particularly upon the relationship between interconnection pricing and the development of competition. I will conclude with some observations on how the development of competition is changing the appropriate method of regulating the industry.

Interconnection Principles

It is a truism that interconnection is central to the development of competition in telecommunications, as it is in other network industries. It is also inevitable that interconnection will be highly controversial. A dominant incumbent benefits from high interconnection prices in two ways. Not only does it gain more revenue, and earn more profit, from higher charges; it also raises its rivals' costs. If competitors are heavy spenders on interconnection, a comparatively small price increase can drive them out of business.

It is therefore not surprising that interconnection prices are a major regulatory battleground, and that all aspects of the process are subject to high inputs of advocacy from interested parties. The scope for this increases because there is no general agreement about the basic principles which should underlie interconnection prices if economic efficiency is to be achieved, let alone about the finer points such as the structure of interconnection pricing and the degree of averaging upon which it should be based. To complicate things further, under an amendment to BT's licence agreed in 1991 as part of the duopoly review, interconnection prices in telecommunications contain an access deficit contribution (ADC) which in certain conditions can be waived.

I consider in turn the economic principles underlying access pricing, the structure of access prices, the appropriate degree of averaging, and the level of access deficit contributions and the waiver.

Setting Access Prices: Two Theories

There are two 'pure' bases for setting access prices, relying respectively on incremental cost and opportunity cost (which in some cases is the same as the stand-alone cost). The argument in favour of incremental costs is the standard one that goods should be traded at or near marginal or incremental cost in order to encourage efficient consumption or use. If this is impossible because of break-even constraints, then attempts should be made to avoid departures from marginal cost pricing of productive inputs such as interconnection services, as such departures cause distortions in the structure of production as well as of consumption.

The most obvious context in which an incremental cost-based interconnection charge would be appropriate is when the service requiring an interconnection input is itself entirely incremental. For example, if mobile services did not compete at all with fixed-link services, mobile should interconnect with the fixed link at incremental costs. This approach has the disadvantage, of course, that it makes the structure of interconnection prices depend upon history, or the order in which new services come along.

The opposite extreme is one in which the service based upon interconnection is substituted one for one for provision by the incumbent. These are the circumstances for which Baumol's efficient component pricing rule (ECPR) seems to be appropriate.[1] Under that rule, the supplier of interconnection services is entitled to charge its rival the sum of its interconnection cost and its opportunity cost, where the latter is defined as the contribution to overheads which the supplier of interconnection services would have made had it continued to sell the output. Under the rule, the supplier of interconnection services effectively has the right to shift its overheads at will on to that part of its output which its rival has to buy, thus freeing it to charge incremental costs in competitive segments.

Limitations of Baumol's Rule

If the only aim of interconnection pricing is cost minimisation at a given level of output and prices, then the efficient component pricing rule is appropriate. An entrant will only come into the market if its total costs can beat the incremental costs of the incumbent in the competitive segment. However, cost minimisation is an appropriate goal only if we assume that competitive entry has no effect either on efficiency or on pricing – in other words, if we assume away the fundamental problems of utility regulation. Baumol himself has been quite explicit about the limitations of his rule, telling the New Zealand High Court (which adopted the rule, although the decision was subsequently overturned on appeal) that ECPR's powers were finite. As he graphically expressed it, 'It does not cure AIDS or baldness'. He assumed, therefore, that other

---

[1] W.J. Baumol, 'Modified Regulation of Telecommunications and the Public Interest Standard', 1991 (mimeo).

techniques such as incentive regulation were capable of ensuring perfectly efficient production and second-best pricing.

But as we are in an imperfect world, optimal interconnection pricing is likely to depend upon the specific circumstances of the case. In particular, there is likely to be a conflict between cost minimisation and allocative efficiency. Following the efficient component pricing rule may ensure production by the lower cost operator, even though that operator may not be efficient. However, it may have the effect of eliminating competition and keeping prices high. In such circumstances, it would be desirable to promote entry in order to put pressure on the incumbent to increase efficiency and, by driving down prices through competition, to promote and improve allocative efficiency. In the limit, this might even imply interconnection prices in the short term below incremental cost. Inconveniently, there is no general rule in the second-best case.

The above is just a preliminary sketch of an argument still in the early stage of development. But if the approach is correct, the regulator must make some kind of judgement about where to position himself or herself upon a quite lengthy continuum. This is definitely not an argument in favour of fully distributed costs, but the latter approach may not be irredeemably irrational, as many economists (myself included) have argued in the past.

Interconnection Practice

In any case, a variant of fully allocated costs is the basis upon which BT's interconnection charges are currently determined, as specified in the licence. This was the approach adopted by Sir Bryan Carsberg when he made his path-breaking BT-Mercury interconnection determination in 1985, and this is the basis upon which the current Director-General, Don Cruickshank, set about the task of redetermining certain terms and conditions of that agreement following a request from both parties in June 1992. The new determination is noted below. First, however, it is useful to note the views about interconnection of several of the parties involved, as expressed in their publicly available responses to OFTEL's statement and consultative paper on separate accounting and interconnection.[2] It is also useful to recall how, under BT's licence conditions, OFTEL is required to address certain aspects of the process, such as access deficit contributions.

---

[2] OFTEL, *Interconnection and Accounting Separation: Consultative Document*, 1993.

The phrasing of BT's licence condition requires that the charges made by BT for anything done under an interconnection agreement should include

> 'fully allocated costs attributable to the services to be provided, taking into account relevant overheads and a reasonable rate of return on attributable assets'.

Many of these terms – notably, 'attributable', 'relevant' and 'reasonable' – are not further defined, so that OFTEL is obliged to make up its own mind on a number of key issues. For example, in establishing a reasonable rate of return, OFTEL has to decide what approach or approaches to adopt; if it adopts an analytical approach such as CAPM (Capital Asset Pricing Model), it has to determine the risk-free rate, the risk premium, the beta of the assets in question and the appropriate gearing level. The recent MMC report on gas[3] illustrates how widely estimates on a reasonable rate of return can vary – ranging from OFGAS's bottom of a range estimate for the transportation business of 1·9 per cent in real terms to BG's proposal of 6·7 per cent (after adjustment for the market-to-assets ratio). OFTEL has to find its way between similarly divergent estimates.

Equally, identification of 'relevant overheads' is likely to be controversial. On an ordinary interpretation, an overhead might be irrelevant to interconnection if it could be attributed to another activity or if it arose from unnecessary expenditure. But this still introduces a major element of judgement.

The 1985 Determination

The condition, however, does not lay down the form of interconnection pricing. The 1985 determination operated by establishing various connection charges and setting out conveyance charges on a per minute basis for local, short national and long national calls, broken down by peak, standard and off-peak. However, a number of respondents to OFTEL's consultation paper, including Mercury and Arthur Andersen, proposed a quite different basis. They suggested that the charging system should be based principally upon busy hour erlangs, on the argument that the principal cost driver for conveyance is the installation of capacity. (This assumption is implicit in the network cost

---

[3] Monopolies and Mergers Commission, *Gas and British Gas plc*, Cm. 2314-17, London: HMSO, 1993.

models developed by Bellcore, for example.) From this perspective, interconnecting operators would be charged on the basis either of their proportionate use of the network during the busy hour, or on the basis of advanced purchase of busy-hour capacity. In addition, there could be a further per minute charge to cover traffic-sensitive costs. This approach could be made quite consistent with fully allocated costs if the appropriate cost data were available. As Arthur Andersen put it:

> 'it is possible to support a wide range of cost allocations, each of which will fall within the bounds of acceptable practice, which will clearly enable different conclusions to be drawn with regard to the calculation of service costs'.

It seems to me, however, that these submissions are drawing too strong an inference from the observation that busy hour erlangs are a major driver of network costs. What we have here is the classic peak-load pricing problem, to which the ordinary rules of analysis apply. That is, if the peak is a fixed one – that is, it is insensitive to the structure of final good prices – and known in advance, then consumers of output produced at peak should bear all the capital costs. If, however, the peak is a shifting one – as is more plausible in tele-communications – then capital costs should be split among consumers of output produced at different times of day in accordance with the strength of their demand.

In other words, it should be possible to translate any interconnection pricing system based upon sharing capacity costs into a precisely equivalent system of time-of-day pricing for interconnection services. To draw a comparison, we would not say that because one of the principal cost drivers in the electricity supply industry is the level of capacity required at peak demand, then all consumers of electricity should contribute directly to the cost of that capacity. It is equally efficient for them to incur the appropriate time-of-day charges for electricity use.

In practice, finding optimal time-of-day prices for interconnection is a particularly difficult problem, as demanders of it – BT and its rivals – are themselves engaged in increasing price competition for final services. As a result, the load factors throughout the day, which in principle should determine interconnection rates, are themselves the outcome of competitive interactions. This makes the equilibrium (if it exists) difficult to compute, but precisely the same difficulty arises in trying to allocate capacity costs directly among the operators.

There is, however, another strand in the argument that the unit of measurement in interconnection should be busy-hour capacity. If this approach were adopted, interconnecting operators would share some of the capital risk of constructing the network. They would also have the flexibility, if they over-bought or under-bought capacity, to reflect their shortages or surpluses in final goods prices. An operator would, moreover, be able to escape from the constraints imposed upon it by BT's structure of retail prices, which at present determines the time bands for interconnection prices. This is a separate but stronger argument for the peak capacity approach.

Interconnection Price Structure in Competitive Markets

More generally, there is a lot to be said for variety and flexibility in access pricing. One way of approaching the issue of how inter-connection pricing might develop in the long term is to speculate about the kind of price structures which might emerge in a competitive infrastructure market. In final service markets in telecoms we observe or expect a variety of non-linear price systems to emerge. Some of these entail substantial fixed charges and low usage charges, while others consist primarily of usage costs. I see no reason why a similar variety of pricing structures would not emerge in a competitive interconnection market. Some customers would want to buy on a per minute basis; others to buy capacity, and assume some of the associated risks and gain flexibility in setting their own tariffs. The latter category might also include resellers of interconnection capacity to other operators. In principle, an appropriate fully allocated cost could be identified according to a number of possible methodologies, although the resulting price schedules might have to be volume-dependent or otherwise complex in order to limit arbitrage. Replicating this hypothetical competitive outcome through regulation would have the consequence for OFTEL of forcing it to undertake several interconnection determinations on several bases at once, but it could be done.

Whatever pricing structure is adopted, the interconnection determination must in practice embody some form of averaging. The alternatives are discussed in OFTEL's Consultative Document.[4] They range from a fully disaggregated actual cost approach, under which an interconnecting operator pays exactly the costs BT incurs in providing interconnection on the route taken for a call, through average

---

[4] *Interconnection and Accounting Separation, op. cit.*

component costs (under which an operator pays the average costs of the components which it purchases) and average function costs (reflecting cost of conveyance between specified parts of the network irrespective of the number of network components used), to tariff-based approaches, under which the charge levied for interconnection is based upon the tariff BT would itself charge for the call, were BT providing it rather than the competitor.

Ignoring the probable impracticability of the first approach, there are two principal issues at stake here. The first concerns the extent to which BT has an incentive to develop its network in various ways, according to the rule adopted. Because the company can reasonably be expected to develop its network to maximise its own benefit, rather than the benefit of all telecommunication operators taken together, this already introduces a possible departure from efficiency. Secondly, the incumbent could in principle, given a particular interconnection rule, construct the network in a way calculated to raise rivals' costs. Although this is a theoretical possibility, because of the inherent difficulties of network design, I am not inclined to regard it as a major problem in practice.

Cost-Based Interconnection Prices?

The second and more serious problem arises from the arbitrary nature of retail prices. Basing interconnection prices on average component or average function costs makes entry profitable in some areas and unprofitable in others. For example, average component charging might lead to relatively high interconnection charges in urban areas, where calls often go through several switches. BT, in its response to the Consultation Paper, suggested that this factor is counterbalanced by relatively high traffic levels, and favours the averaging of interconnection prices on the basis of costs, rather than any linkage between interconnection charges and retail prices. Competition optimists (of whom I am one) believe that entry will fairly soon sort out the worst imbalances between costs and prices. For this reason, it would be a retrograde step to sacrifice rational interconnection prices on the altar of current retail tariffs, even if the pain of rebalancing may have to be spread over a period.

But this issue goes further than the method of averaging. The current interconnection determination sets rates geared essentially to BT's retail charging structure. If this is maintained, other operators tend to be drawn to the same structure, as a major part of their costs is determined by BT's pricing decisions. In the medium term, it should prove possible to cut this tie by progressive disaggregation of cost-based prices, and by more flexible arrangements for selling interconnection services.

Access Deficit Contributions

The last, but certainly not the least, aspect of the new interconnection determination concerns access deficit contributions. Interconnection charges may now embody a contribution made by the interconnecting operator to BT's access deficit, unless the ADC is waived by the Director-General. The ADC of a call minute is proportional to the profitability of that call type for BT; accordingly, it is much higher for an international call minute than for a local call minute.

The procedure which OFTEL goes through is as follows. First, it calculates BT's access deficit, drawing on information from the company's financial returns by service. It then has to decide whether BT is providing access services efficiently. If the conclusion is that it is not, OFTEL can reduce BT's access costs by a maximum of 5 per cent, although reducing allowable access costs by 5 per cent reduces the access deficit by more than 10 per cent (on 1990/91 data). The resulting deficit is then allocated across call minutes in proportion to their profitability. Finally, the Director-General has the power to waive access deficit contributions in certain cases.

One of the key conditions determining the availability of a waiver relates to the market shares of BT and any entrant. The DGT can grant a full or partial waiver on a market share of up to 10 per cent held by a single firm. If, however, BT's market share falls below 85 per cent, no further waivers can be offered. Presumably, entrants' own direct provision of services falls within the market definition so that a proportion of any waiver accrues to traffic where no contribution is due.

It is obvious that the definition of a market plays a key rôle in this elaborate process. Broadly, BT would like markets to be defined as narrowly as possible, precluding a waiver over as much as possible of its business, while entrants would like market shares to be defined as widely as possible, thus delaying the attainment of the 10 and 15 per cent thresholds.

Defining the Telecoms Market: 'a Regulatory Minefield'

The analytical resolution of this issue is highly complex. It is well known that the appropriate way of defining a market hinges critically upon the use to which the definition will be put. The function of the access deficit waiver is to enable firms to overcome problems created by economies of scale and handicaps associated with such things as the lack of number portability. This implies that the production character- istics of various services are relevant. It seems to me, therefore, that a plausible case can be made for distinguishing domestic and inter- national telecommunications markets, as the latter require distinctive production facilities.

But this is clearly a regulatory minefield, and it is useful to review how other regulators have tackled the definitional question. The Aust- ralian Bureau of Transport and Communications Economics has conducted a valuable survey of international market definitions.[5] It notes that the US Federal Communications Commission (FCC) con- cluded in 1980 that the appropriate geographic area for the domestic long-distance telecommunications market was the continental United States, rather than individual city payers. However, this leaves open the question of whether local and long-distance services are in the same market. In relation to Australia, the Bureau concluded that there are separate markets for domestic and international telecommunication services, and that individual country pairs should also be treated as separate markets. It also noted that there is some analytical support for separating local and trunk markets in Australia. The difficulty with the latter position is that, especially in a smaller area like the UK, network developments are increasingly eroding the distinction between local and long-distance.

This catalogue of decisions which have to be taken by the regulator in order to make an interconnection determination and implement the procedures for access deficit contributions is intended to demonstrate that the present system is at the limits of workability. It entails a whole series of discretionary judgements about BT's efficiency, the definition of markets and the necessity or legitimacy of waivers. Perhaps most objectionably, it requires the Director-General to divide a limited amount of waivers among an unknown number of actual or potential competitors. Under the duopoly, the arrangement might have made some kind of sense, but it seems out of place in the present increasingly competitive world.

---

[5] Bureau of Transport and Communications Economics, *The Australian Telecommunications Market: When Does Dominance Cease?*, Working Paper 6, BTCE, 1992.

Rebalancing to Replace ADCs?

What might take the place of the access deficit contributions? The simple answer is that to permit rebalancing would eliminate the need for them. Freeing BT from its RPI+2 constraint on quarterly rentals would place it in the interesting position of having to decide what degree of rebalancing is appropriate in the new competitive circumstances. But given the potential impact of fully allocated cost pricing on residential bills, the experiment might prove politically disastrous.

My preferred alternative is as follows. One of the problems of the present ADC system is that it aims to compensate BT for the deficit it incurs – compared with fully allocated costs – in the provision of access. Yet access is pretty meaningless by itself, as its utility is wholly dependent upon the expectation of use. A more satisfactory procedure in the long run would be to identify the costs imposed by *loss-making customers* and share them. Australian experience has illustrated that calculation of the net cost of universal service obligations is a difficult but practicable task.[6] The European Commission, in its recent draft proposals on the funding of universal service obligations (USOs) in the newly liberalised markets, appears to be moving in the same direction. Since the cost of USOs is likely to be substantially less than the access deficit, the need for waivers would be much reduced. I recognise that the purpose of ADCs – to discourage inefficient entry – is rather different from that of sharing universal service costs, which arise from requiring tariffs to be averaged. In the medium term the need for ADCs should disappear as rebalancing is allowed, but the need for an equitable allocation of universal service costs is likely to be much more durable. The switch I am proposing would go some way towards meeting the medium-term objective while at the same time laying the groundwork for a longer-term system of sharing USO costs.

More generally, in the longer term, interconnection pricing should be less subject to regulatory discretion but more flexible in structure. Ideally, as many prices as possible would be determined through market negotiation. It is implausible, however, that regulatory involvement will disappear altogether: the conflicts of interest are too great. However, the process could clearly be streamlined by the availability of a menu of standard prices, possibly constructed on alternative bases. Given the doubts about appropriate principles for pricing intercon-

---

[6] Bureau of Transport and Communications Economics, *The Cost of Telecoms' Community Service Obligations*, Report 64, BTCE, 1989.

nection services, it seems to me that continued reliance upon a fully allocated cost ceiling is an imperfect but workable compromise.

Separate Accounting

Where does separate accounting fit into all of this? So far I have focussed upon the regulatory pricing of interconnection because I see that as the fundamental method of facilitating efficient competition in the market. Except in one important respect noted below, the value added of separate accounting is to provide a monitoring device, through the disclosure of 'excess' returns on potentially monopolistic assets or inadequate returns on competitive services using monopolistic inputs. The problem with the procedure is that the regulatory feedback loop is long term and uncertain. It may take several years for a pattern of excess returns to be identified; moreover, such an identification requires an estimate of the cost of capital to the relevant assets. Thus while separate accounting *per se* can add something, it would be unwise to place too much reliance upon it. In this connection it is interesting to note that both BT and Mercury (although not other respondents to the consultation paper) took the view that the full panoply of separate accounting proposed by OFTEL is unnecessary, and that it is preferable simply to account separately for the local loop.

Separate accounting has an important corollary, however, when BT is required to equate interconnection prices and its own transfer prices. OFTEL has stated that it will require BT not to discriminate between itself and other operators in setting network charges for special offers. The precise form of the licence condition will be important here, particularly as it relates to the length of time over which network charges should be averaged. BT's data suggest that the special offers have had considerable effects on demand, with price elasticities four or five times higher than estimates derived from time-series data. The issue is therefore an important one, though distinct in principle from separate accounting.

Regulated Competition

I noted at the outset that the months since mid-1993 have seen important developments in competition. Moreover, with the exception of the international market where regulatory exclusions still persist, competition has come to all market segments. Subscribers to telephony provided by cable television operators have multiplied, and radio-based technologies are now invading the local loop – providers of both fixed service such as Ionica, and mobile services such as Mercury One-2-One and Metro and Euro Digital.

The interesting feature of these developments is that they entail competition between technologies with different cost structures. Fixed-link technologies are characterised by very high non-traffic-sensitive costs in laying down the network, and relatively low traffic-sensitive costs. In the case of radio-based technologies, however, the traffic-sensitive component is much higher. This arises because the size of the cell can, within certain limits, be varied in accordance with expected traffic volumes. A second consideration is that spectrum requirements are traffic sensitive, so that any attempts to introduce spectrum charges, as are now occurring in the United States, would increase the weight of usage costs in total costs.

The natural expectation in such cases is that customers will segment themselves according to the cost structures of the operators, which themselves would be reflected in their tariffs. Thus a wire-based technology, with substantial access costs and low usage costs, would be especially attractive to high users, whilst wireless technologies, with low access but high usage charge, would attract low users.

How this turns out in practice depends upon the degree to which the wireless operators can get their costs down and the extent to which customers rate the extra mobility of the new operators, compared with the limited coverage of their services. However, there is already evidence that the new operators are breaking away from the straitjacket of BT's price structures to which Mercury's fixed-link service has hitherto been confined. This reinforces the argument noted above for greater flexibility in the structure of interconnection prices.

At the same time, the growth in the availability of telecommunications services provides competition for BT at the other end of the cost structure. Cable companies provide relatively few lines, but their number is growing quickly. The US evidence suggests that the costs of building a new broad-band cable system are high, so that at UK penetration levels for entertainment, operators have to succeed in telecommunications as well to break even. This provides a strong incentive.

BT's plans to offer video on demand may interfere with the cable companies' penetration in entertainment. But they have to overcome technical hurdles as well as demonstrating that video on demand is regarded by households as an appropriate substitute for a multi-channel cable system. (I note in passing that they create interesting problems for access pricing, as OFTEL may be asked to allocate conveyance costs between the simultaneous delivery down a copper pair of both a video and a telephone message.) The prospects still look reasonable for wire-based competition.

Conclusion: OFTEL's Expanding Work-Load

The implications for OFTEL of multiple entry are enormous. At the simple work-load level, the office is now responsible for monitoring 40 or so licences, instead of the handful in existence during the duopoly policy. The number of possible interconnection arrangements grows with the square of the number of licensees, so that some kind of streamlining or standardisation is necessary. But, more importantly, the style of regulation has to change. The duopoly policy entailed regulation according to a blueprint, the principal element of which was the survival of Mercury. To that extent it was outcome-driven. With multiple entry, the regulator cannot work to a blueprint of market structure or market shares. The regulatory system has to be as symmetrical as possible, or at least even-handed among non-dominant operators. Thus I have argued above that the notion of favouring particular operators through the granting of waivers is not really sustainable (and indeed will come to an end in 1997 when waivers can no longer be granted).

In a recent book, extolling the virtues of wireless, George Calhoun set out a vision of a new world of telecommunications which he described as 'laminated access network' or a 'laminar network'.[7] In Calhoun's words, this is a world in which 'multiple carriers provide complementary, somewhat differentiated, overlapping access fabrics'. He goes on to argue that all competitive markets are laminar, as they all involve multiple overlapping distribution structures aimed at the same population base. He predicts competition between and within technologies, based upon product differentiation. Customers will typically be attached to a number of interlocking networks.

In the UK, this vision is now much more plausible than it was in 1991. But its realisation depends crucially upon interconnection. If the current public debates can resolve that problem, they will have gone a long way to create conditions for achieving this competitive vision.

---

[7] G. Calhoun, *Wireless Access and the Local Telephone Network*, Boston, Mass.: Artech House, 1992.

Postscript

In December 1993, the Director-General of Telecommunications issued his determination of interconnection charges between British Telecom and Mercury.[8] The determination and the accompanying explanatory document indicated the DGT's views on many of the issues discussed above. In particular, the determination:

o Established new rates for Mercury to connect with BT's system and new rates for the conveyance of calls for Mercury by BT. These were based upon fully allocated costs, but in making the calculations OFTEL excluded as irrelevant certain categories of expenditure such as indirect advertising, 'blue skies' research, certain restructuring costs and the costs of the Chairman's office and associated activities.

o OFTEL also calculated access deficit contributions for each type of call. These depend upon profitability of the service in question, and range from 0·27p per minute for a local call at cheap rate to 58·01p per minute for the most profitable international calls at peak rate. In calculating the access deficit contributions, the DGT decided that BT's access deficit did not require adjustment on the grounds that the company was providing the service less efficiently than comparable operators in the USA.

o In interpreting the conditions under which access deficit contributions can be waived, the DGT indicated that he divided telecommunications markets into national and international markets. He determined that Mercury should have a full waiver on the first 10 per cent of its share of the market in local and national calls taken together, and a full waiver on the first 10 per cent of its share of the market in international calls. These decisions would be reviewed in 1995 and 1994 respectively. An accompanying statement of policy indicated the basis upon which waivers of access deficit contribution would be made in future. These include a

---

[8] OFTEL, *Determination of Terms and Conditions for the Purpose of an Agreement on the Interconnection of the British Telecommunications System and the Mercury Communications Ltd. System Under Condition 13 of the Licence Granted to British Telecommunications Under Section 7 of the Telecommunications Act 1984, Interconnection Charges: An Explanatory Document*, 1993.

consideration of the extent to which companies seeking a waiver would be providing competition to BT in the local loop, particularly in providing services to residential customers.

CHAIRMAN'S COMMENTS

William Wigglesworth
OFTEL

I SHOULD HAVE PREFACED Martin's remarks by saying that he wished it to be made clear that his remarks were purely personal, and were not made in any way on behalf of OFTEL, or in relation to OFTEL, and that applies even more in the case of my own comments. I would like to emphasise that naturally they will be even more bland, but I would like to emphasise that nothing should be inferred from my remarks relating to the plethora of interconnect and access waiver decisions currently before OFTEL.

Thank you also, Martin, for letting me have a sight of an earlier draft of your paper. This turned out to be something of a poisoned chalice because, of course, you did not stick to your paper at all, and, having geared my notes to your paper, I found myself slightly adrift. But we very much agree on our approach. I find myself in some difficulty in finding issues on which to disagree, or even much alter emphasis. We share the perception of the importance of the issues.

Interconnection the Dominant Issue

I remember years ago, when the liberalisation process was starting, Sir Keith Joseph, as he then was, came back from the United States with a phrase that he had been told: 'It all comes down to interconnection'. And at the time we were not really quite sure what interconnection was, though we later found out. And by 1983, when I was back in the field of telecommunications, the issues were then firmly in the 'too difficult to answer' tray, and I am afraid I left them there. And it was not until 1985, when Sir Bryan Carsberg masterminded the BT-Mercury determination, that we really got to grips with the issues and their solutions.

Since then, interconnection has been a dominant issue. Currently it, and a whole range of related issues, particularly the associated barriers to entry, are at the top of OFTEL's agenda. Clearly, satisfactory arrangements for interconnect are central to enabling fully effective network competition to develop. And we share perceptions of the complexity following the enormous response to the Duopoly Review. The present arrangements do seem to be at the limits of practicability, even perhaps beyond them, and already it seems impossible to find a solution that is entirely acceptable to all players, either in, or about to be in, the market. New competitors are unlikely to be receptive to the view that the Pareto-optimisation principle, which appeared in your draft paper, requires them to go out of business! And they are clear that they want a reasonable degree of assurance that the regulatory arrangements on which they enter the market will continue.

Dynamic Effects of Entry

The pro-competitive regulator, in the search for rules to apply to facilitate efficient competition and a reasonable balance of competitive parity is most likely, it seems to me, to be concerned with the dynamic effects of the entry he is promoting. This sort of question concerns how quickly one can expect an efficient new entrant to be able to take on the might of a total monopolist, if it has to connect at the incumbent's inflated costs, or costs inflated later. And, faced with developing efficient competition, how quickly will the incumbent reduce its costs to the level that the new entrants should have been paying all along?

To capture these effects, I am inclined to think in terms of biological analogies of organisms. I used to think this was an original approach, until I found that the great Professor Hayek had trained as a biologist and routinely presented his ideas in this way. And now it is all the rage: Bruno Lasarre, the French telecom regulator, likens his functions to gardening, and compares the formal gardening on the French model with the luxuriant garden, not to say jungle, that has been encouraged to develop in Britain.

The gardener, at least the British one, is well aware that his seeds need warm, moist soil to begin with, but then need hardening off before facing the full rigours of the British climate. Something of the same approach seems likely to be necessary to encourage taking the investment and other risks concerned in market entry. And so I was particularly encouraged to hear you suggest the tempering of the harsh Baumol rules of efficient component pricing in respect of new entrants. They do not seem to cater very well for the case where a competitor is building a network that turns out, after all, to be more efficient than the incumbent – an incumbent who is first able to add 'opportunity costs' when the competitor is still building, and then reduce market prices when full competition arrives. This seems uncomfortably like getting one's cake and eating it.

At the other end of the cost spectrum, I have to admit to being very much in sympathy with the incremental cost approach. The first business that I managed was a plant bakery which enjoyed excellent economies of scale, so long as it was at over 85 per cent of capacity. Provided everyone was careful, there were good profits to be made and competitors to be hurt at that level of capacity by picking up sizeable wholesale customers at considerable discounts. I was very conscious of those incremental costs and their effects. So my question to the accountant with the sharp pencil was always: 'What is the effect on next week's bottom line?'.

Back in 1985 in telecoms, we were certainly very aware of the amount of spare capacity on BT's network, and its impact on the costs of handling limited amounts of new traffic in various locations. There was, perhaps, more of an element of incremental costing about the judgements then made than was widely realised at the time. It would no doubt have been better had we been able to publish more information then, as we are now doing. Though I would not, of course, depart from your assessment that fully allocated cost has been, and remains, the basis of the determination of interconnect charges. And I support what I take to be your inference that this has so far not turned out in practice too badly, though I accept that the future looks rather different.

I was particularly interested in your remarks about the suggestions of Arthur Andersen, among others, that interconnect pricing should relate to the proportion of use of the network during the busy hour. It has always surprised me that the telecommunications industry has not so far used load-factor pricing on the electricity model, despite the fact that many of the accountants concerned at one time moved across from electricity. One reason may be that electricity facilities tend to blow up in conditions of overload, whereas telephone networks merely fail to provide dial tone or give the engaged tone, if overloaded. It is a concept that certainly seems well worth considering. I can see it could lead to increased complexity, and I am not sure how far peak capacity demand in practice equates to incremental cost, or how it would impact on new entrants, particularly in a multi-operator environment. I entirely agree with your view that some form of averaging is inevitable, and with your preference for rational interconnect prices, though this may be easier said than done.

75

Problems of ADCs

I thought you were extremely diplomatic about the problems of Access Deficit Contributions, and the granting of waivers, which I too regard as a means of reducing the barriers to entry that, for the best of reasons, have been created by delaying the rate at which BT can rebalance fixed charges and usage charges. I also strongly endorse your distinction between intended compensation of BT's alleged access deficit, via access deficit contributions, and the issue of sharing the cost of genuinely loss-making customers. For this provision is made in BT's licence, by the raising of access charges. This distinction is one that is not always made in discussion; it should be remembered.

I was, however, a bit disappointed at what I felt to be a somewhat dismissive tone on accounting separation. The issue here, it seems to me, is assisting the opening of the market, first, by providing BT's competitors with the assurance that they are being treated in the same way as BT treats the part of its business that the competitor is facing. I think there is a competition feedback as well as a regulatory feedback. Secondly, it reinforces what I would regard as the inevitable requirement for large, vertically integrated firms trading in different markets, where their competitors are their largest customers, to develop clear transfer price policies to ensure that both parts of their own business can compete effectively. Regulation here is trying to move in the same direction as the market will move. Indeed, there are already some market signs of this in BT's relations with the cable companies, in whose interconnection business BT is clearly interested.

Finally, I was encouraged by, and in full agreement with, your upbeat approach to the prospects for successful entry, and the creation of a multiple network environment. Your vision of overlapping and competing networks is becoming a familiar one, and I think a convincing one. It set me thinking how far, as a lower-cost modern technology is introduced by competing operators, the problems of interconnect will fall away as market entry succeeds on a large scale, both at long distance and local level. If this does indeed happen, the present complexities and difficulties of interconnection can clearly be seen as a transitional phase, and it should not be beyond the wit of man or regulator to devise arrangements that will take us into conditions of fully effective telecommunications competition.

5

REGULATING NETWORKS

Professor John Kay
London Economics

What Is a Network?

MY SUBJECT IS THE ISSUE of regulating networks. Let me begin by defining the main characteristics of what I mean by a network. The service which a network provides involves transportation of a good, a service, or a commodity from one point to another. A network achieves this by means of general facilities which are provided in common for all possible users, rather than ones which are dedicated to each individually. Thus we think of an electricity grid, or a gas pipeline, as a network. Although trucks provide transport and so do cars, the individual nature of the service they provide distinguishes them, although of course they may use a road network in delivering that service. We recognise networks across all utilities – telecommunications, gas, electricity, water, transport services by road and rail. The concept can be extended to include other activities, such as exchanges that clear financial transactions.

Degrees of Homogeneity

Although all networks have a range of common features, there is one important differentiating characteristic, which depends on how homogeneous the product shipped across the network is. Electricity and railways are at the extreme ends of the spectrum. Each day the number of people who wish to travel from Birmingham to London is very much the same as the number of people who wish to travel from London to Birmingham. It is, however, impossible to net out the numbers in each direction and simply ship the resulting balance, so saving a great deal of money. However, this is precisely what happens in electricity.

77

Electricity is such a homogeneous product that it is fundamentally meaningless to ask whose electricity it is which any particular user consumes. In rail and telecommunications, on the other hand, you produce the product yourself and ask the network provider to ship it. Gas and water lie somewhere in between. I shall come back later to some of the implications of this issue.

Regulatory Issues: Allocating Costs to Users

A variety of regulatory issues are common to all networks. One important one is that there is, in principle, actually a different cost for providing every individual service to every individual user. These costs depend not only on the nature of the user's demand, but on the time of day and on the use that other people are making of the network at that particular time. It is obviously impracticable to tailor charges as elaborately as this, and no network does so. Customers are charged a figure that relates to the average of a group of similar users.

However, since most networks are not subject to competitive pressures – they are often natural monopolies and this has frequently been reinforced by statutory monopoly as well – such averaging has typically gone far beyond what is required by technical practicability. There have often been political pressures to do this. So British Gas charges a uniform price to domestic users across the country. Charges for the use of the national grid are more or less unrelated to the nature of the specific carriage provided.

'Top-Down' and 'Bottom-Up'

The regulatory implications of this averaging can only be appreciated if it is first known what the costs attributable to uses or users are. This can be done either on a 'top-down' basis, in which the aggregate costs of operating the network are assigned to individual uses or individual users. Or it can be done on a 'bottom-up' basis. Here the objective is to identify the specific costs imposed on the network by individual users, or by particular activities.

Commonly, there are huge differences between the answers which are reached by these two methods. The top-down attribution of costs comes up with answers which are far larger than the bottom-up measurement of costs. The general response is to invent some concept, called access, or network services, or availability, or use of resources, to fill the gap. My objective here is to focus on that issue, and to approach the problem as a general one across the whole set of network industries. I wish to query whether these elusive items – access, availability, resources – really exist, or at least to suggest that they are rather small.

Incremental Costs and Tariff Averaging Under Competition

The combination of incremental costs that are apparently very low and extensive averaging of tariffs raised few practical difficulties so long as networks remained monopolies. As competition has been introduced, both averaging and low reported incremental costs have raised key issues for all regulators. Competition is attracted wherever there are large divergences between prices and costs. The correct regulatory objective is to ensure that competition emerges where the competitor is more efficient than the incumbent, and not otherwise. But the practical reality is that nearly all the competition which has been introduced in British utilities in the last decade has been induced by tariff distortion rather than by the greater efficiency of the entrant.

I am not in any way here seeking to criticise the efforts which have been made to introduce competition or to decry its success. The development of this competition has had desirable effects on improving the efficiency of incumbents. But competition is almost entirely the result of discrepancies between prices and costs, rather than excessive *levels* of costs, and competition has been directed at the areas where the margins between prices and costs are highest. That is why Mercury has focussed on international and long-distance calls, and on some other business services. That is why competition in the electricity industry has nothing whatever to do with differences in the costs of generation or supply. The same is true of the tariff negotiation that is suddenly emerging in the water industry.

The issues I am describing – what are the costs of supplying services and uses and how do we bridge the gap between incremental costs and average costs – are common to all network industries. The principles I want to enunciate in this paper apply also to all of these industries. But I wish to focus on the way the problem has emerged in two particular sectors. Both of these are matters of considerable current controversy and will serve to illustrate both my points and the importance of the issues involved. One of these concerns interconnect charges in telecommunications. The other is the question of inset appointments and negotiation of charges in the water industry. Those of you who are concerned with gas, with electricity transmission, or with rail track charges will recognise that the same issues arise in these industries in slightly modified forms.

Telecom Interconnect and Water Inset Problems

Let me outline the main elements of the specific problems of telecom interconnect and water inset. It has been evident ever since the first stirrings of competition in telecommunications that the terms on which entrants would be allowed access to the incumbent's network were critical. In 1985 Oftel made an important determination of these terms in respect of Mercury. Now, however, with many more PTOs, each with different types of demand for access, the issue has to be thought through again in a much wider context. The result has been a consultative paper which Oftel is now discussing with interested parties.

The problems with which I am concerned today emerge clearly in the consultative paper. The dichotomy is raised explicitly in terms of the acknowledged tension which exists between Licence Condition 13, which allows BT to recover from its access customers the fully allocated costs of the services they receive, and Licence Condition 17A, which allows BT to price at incremental cost. The problem can also be seen, more importantly but less precisely, by reference to a loosely defined concept of 'network services'.

The licences, or strictly speaking appointments, of water companies give them monopolies in their areas of supply, but in 1992 the possibility of 'inset appointments' was created. The holder of an inset appointment, who might be another company but might equally be the customer himself, is entitled to a bulk supply from his local water company. The possibility of such inset appointments gives the first opportunity for customers to negotiate prices with their suppliers. Within the last few months, ICI and Gatwick Airport have, on this basis, achieved substantial price reductions from their current suppliers, and the queue of customers wishing to embark on such discussions is rapidly lengthening. Ofwat has recently produced guidance on how to deal with such negotiations in the form of a letter, RD 9. This letter suggests, broadly speaking, that those who are connected to a general network should pay the average costs of supply within that network, while those who are not connected – those who have essentially independent supplies – should pay the costs of their individual supply. It is clear that this is very far from the end of the story. For the first time in the history of the water sector, the industry has to think through the issue of identifying the cost of supplying each of its customers.

Incremental and Total Costs – Theory

What I should like to do here is to explain some simple theory on the borders between economics and accounting that underpins these problems and, in particular that theory which relates to the differences between average and incremental cost. On the basis of that analysis, I wish to propose a general regulatory strategy for dealing with the questions I have raised which I believe has relevance right across the utility sector.

Let me begin with a fundamental proposition in economics and accounting. It is that there are only two reasons why the sum of incremental costs can fall short of total costs. The first is that there are economies of scale and scope in the provision of network services. The second is that some of the activities concerned are not performed efficiently. The corollary is that in the absence of these reasons – that is, if there are no scale or scope economies and the range of activities in the network is optimally provided, the sum of the incremental costs of providing a service to each individual user will be equal to the total costs incurred. The importance of this proposition is that it both defines and limits the possibility that incremental costs can fail to recover overall required revenues.

A further corollary of this proposition is that the amount of the difference between the total of incremental costs and aggregate costs is equal to the aggregate of the costs of such inefficiency and the sum of the value of the scale and scope economies. There is also a useful result that incremental costs, measured as a percentage of total costs, will be equal to the elasticity of costs with respect to output. It is important to understand the force of the latter observation. If that elasticity were to be 0·8, it would mean that marginal costs would equal 80 per cent of average costs. If the elasticity were to be 0·8, it would also mean that a firm three times the size would have costs only half as great. Similarly, economies of scope of that magnitude would imply that a firm undertaking three related activities would be able to do them all at half the cost. In short, it would be impossible for competition to exist in an industry in which scale or scope economies were as extensive as that. The implication is that unless scale or scope economies are massive, or alternatively inefficiency is enormous, the gap between incremental costs and average costs cannot be very great.

The question that then faces us is why the differences that are typically identified in practice seem to be so large. In telecoms, for example, we are told that there have been difficulties in attributing more than 20 per cent of the costs of the business directly to specific users. There are two other reasons why the gap between average and incremental costs is commonly found to be substantial, each of which has to do with errors in calculation rather than the technical characteristics of the business. The accounting conventions employed in calculating marginal costs differ from those employed in the calculation of average costs. In particular, average costs are very often based on the historic cost of assets while marginal or incremental costs reflect the costs of new or replacement activities.

The second reason, and I believe in practice by far the most important, is that the errors which are made in 'bottom-up' calculations are precisely the opposite of those which are made in 'top-down' calculations. Errors in the bottom-up approach are almost always errors of exclusion – too many things are left out. Errors in the top-down approach are almost always errors of inclusion – too many things are left in.

Incremental and Average Cost Differences

Taken as a whole, then, that gives us four reasons for differences between incremental and average costs – economies of scale and scope, inefficiency, accounting mismatches, and errors of inclusion and exclusion. I shall discuss these in turn.

(i) Economies of Scale and Scope

Discussion of scale and scope economies in networks is particularly difficult and particularly confused. As far as economies of scale are concerned, the size of the network as such yields almost no scale economies. For example, if British Telecom and France Telecom amalgamated, the costs of running the two networks together would be virtually indistinguishable from the costs of running them separately. Homogeneous product networks are different. There are economies of scale in increasing the aggregate size of an electricity grid because you can provide supply security at lower cost. That is why the French and British electricity grids are linked, although by the time networks have reached the size of either the benefits of further extension are quite small.

More usually, there are *scale* economies in *use* of the network, achieved by using a network more intensively. Providing and laying a pipe with twice the capacity does not as a rule cost twice as much, and very often you do not need twice the pipe for twice the volume anyway. These economies of scale in network use are large in little-used branches of the network, such as individual supply pipes or telephone lines, but are generally small in heavily used ones, such as international or inter-city telephone calls, or main distribution pipes.

The main source of economies of *scope* is the ability to net off flows in networks where the product shipped through it is homogeneous. Much less transmission needs to be done in a large electricity grid than would be needed if the same grid were fragmented. This happens because flows in one direction can be balanced against flows in another. In rail transport, or in telecoms, where such netting is impossible, scope economies are quite low. Scope economies are, therefore, of moderate size in water and small in telecoms.

(ii) Efficiency Issues

Let me turn now to efficiency issues. These are of two kinds. The first is that utilities have a legacy of over-manning. When average costs are computed, these are necessarily built in; when incremental costs are measured, it is generally assumed that best practice will be achieved. The existence of this difference creates the question of who should bear the costs of failing to achieve best practice and, conversely, who should benefit from their elimination.

The second type of inefficiency is where there is excess or inadequate capacity within a network. Excess capacity is the most common. If capacity is inefficiently large, incremental costs will be below average costs, while where there are capacity shortages average costs will be below incremental costs. In the water industry, the range of incremental costs of water supply is, for this reason, very large. It is very low, for example, in parts of the north of England, where the massive under-utilised resources of Kielder Water are determined by the high costs of substantial new investment. In telecoms, over- or under-capacity rarely lasts for long because of the rate of underlying growth of demand.

These two things together, inefficiency and scale and scope economies, explain some of the differences between average and incremental costs. But most of the explanation is to be found elsewhere.

(iii) Accounting Mismatches

I begin with those which arise from differences in accounting conventions. Incremental cost calculations are, by their very nature, related to current cost accounting principles. Average cost calculations, on the other hand, are normally based on historic cost. In most circumstances, current costs will be above historic costs by virtue of inflation. Mismatches of accounting convention should therefore help to eliminate any divergences between average and incremental costs which arise from my first two sources of difference, since they tend to increase incremental costs relative to average costs. The position in the two industries I am discussing, however, is more complex than this. Telecoms is one of the few industries in which current cost is frequently below historic cost because of the extraordinary rate of technical progress. Water is very much the other way around. We need only think, if we can bear to do so, of London sewers. Historic cost mostly incurred a century ago is trivial. Current cost is unimaginably large.

There is a further complicating factor. Water companies were sold at prices far below the current cost valuation of their assets. This creates what has been commonly described as 'the customer share'. That customer share holds down prices to customers below the average levels which current cost principles would dictate. This means that average costs, in which the customer share is to be included, are low. But it would not seem appropriate to include a customer share and hence write down the cost of capital in measuring *incremental* costs in the water industry. Thus, the way in which customers who wish to seek inset appointments or obtain bulk supplies should benefit from the customer share, and if they should benefit from it at all, is one of the issues which is raised by inset appointments.

(iv) Errors of Inclusion and Exclusion

But the fourth explanation is the most important. It is the difference between the results obtained from top-down and bottom-up calculations. As I have already suggested, top-down calculations are typically characterised by errors of inclusion; there are more costs included than are properly attributable to individual customers. As far as bottom-up calculations are concerned, these are typically characterised by errors of exclusion – we forget to put things in, or do not properly realise that additional expenditures of many kinds may be required if additional supplies are to be provided.

An important development in accounting theory and practice in the last decade has been the growth of systems of activity-based costing. These provide a link between economic and accounting approaches to issues of cost allocation and measurement. They also clarify considerably the relationships between incremental and average costs. The essence of activity-based costing is to insist on causality in relation to *all* cost attribution.

For those who are not familiar with this kind of approach, let me illustrate what it means. The archetype of what is typically treated as an overhead cost and attributed on some arbitrary criteria is an item like the chairman's salary. In the case of British Telecom, at least, this amount is sufficiently significant for some care to be required over its attribution. The problem we face is that if we ask how much time does the chairman of British Telecom give to worrying about the supply of telephone service to line 071-436-2991 (London Economics), the answer is none whatever. And the same is true for all other individual customers of BT. That means that it is virtually impossible to identify any part of this overall cost with any particular customer.

However, once one starts to look behind this and seek chains of causality, the position is rather different. We have to begin by asking what it is that the chairman actually does. That is not a wise question to pose in most organisations, including London Economics. Perhaps the chairman spends part of his time talking to shareholders. If he does so, then presumably the reason is in order to enable equity financing to be obtained more cheaply, and therefore the time he spends on this is properly a cost of raising equity finance. Equally, he may spend part of his time motivating employees. Presumably, the rationale of this is that they are likely to work harder or more effectively as a result and one would add such costs to the direct wage costs of the individuals concerned. Or the chairman may spend part of his time looking for new business opportunities for the firm. This is an entirely proper activity for him to engage in, but one which is clearly not attributable or chargeable to the existing customers of the business. And so on... . By introducing activities, which form the link between the overhead functions of the business and the actual services provided, we can achieve specific attribution of virtually all of the costs of the firm concerned.

The essential point is that, seen within this framework, all cost analysis is focussed on the purpose of the expenditure. Once we have determined the purpose for which an expenditure is incurred, we can trace the costs through to the particular services which lead these costs to be incurred. The corollary – and this is important – is that if a causal linkage related to the supply of particular services cannot be established, then the regulator must take the view that the cost is not one which is properly incurred, or at least properly chargeable to the regulated customers.

Now, in London Economics there are sensible limits to how far we are willing to take activity-based costing. It would clearly not be cost effective to require that the chairman's day be divided into intervals of one minute, but one would wish to break it down into broad categories. In BT, on the other hand, where the accounting function is large and the importance of getting precise answers to these questions very considerable, one might reasonably ask for a very high proportion of costs to be allocated by means of activity-based costing. Once we are down to the last one or two per cent, we might allow general attribution, but not before that.

Some of you may think that this is not so different from the exercises of cost allocation that accountants generally engage in. Let me make clear that it is not. Few conventional accounting systems and structures emerge well when judged in this light. The clearest indication of allocation systems that take inadequate account of causality occurs where a significant proportion of costs are allocated on bases which are either *pro rata* to the revenues of the firm or *pro rata* to other costs which are susceptible to direct measurement. You will recognise that the vast majority of cost allocation systems do in practice attribute many costs on one or other of these bases. This is a clear sign of what I think of as lazy accountancy, and of a failure to determine the causality involved, because there are almost no costs in any business which are directly proportional either to the amount of revenues or to the quantum of direct costs. Credit risk and financing costs are virtually the only expenditures which are directly driven by volume of revenues.

In general, obtaining more revenue for the same service or activity involves no higher costs. Similarly, there are almost no indirect costs which are *causally* related to the volume of direct costs. Examples which do meet this criterion are social security payments, which are broadly proportional to wages. Pension contributions are similarly proportional. It is perfectly clear, on the other hand, that the chairman's motivating effect on employees is not causally related to the amount that the employees in question are paid. There can be, therefore, no justification for any substantial part of costs being allocated proportionally to revenues or to direct costs in an activity-based costing system. These methods of allocation result from a failure to think properly about causality.

A Strategy for Regulators

Let me go on to put forward a strategy for regulators confronted by these issues. It follows from my argument that if the exercise of cost allocation is undertaken properly, it will be possible to determine incremental costs of the whole range of services which networks provide and that we should not expect that there will be large differences between the aggregate of these incremental costs and the total costs which are incurred by the business. I have suggested that the reasons for the differences which emerge in practice are in part the results of poor accounting practice and in part the results of genuine underlying problems. I believe the first job of the regulator is to eliminate those discrepancies which result from poor accounting practice. That means that most regulated activities should be accounted for on a current cost basis. The case for this is, in any event, strong. It establishes a direct connection between regulated charges and the price level which would prevail in a competitive market. It also means that regulated industries should be required to adopt accounting systems which make full use of activity-based costing systems and which ensure that the vast majority of their costs are specifically identified with the provision of specific customer services. I understand the regulatory despair which is engendered, particularly in Oftel, at its failure to achieve this result even after 10 years of discussing BT's methods of cost attribution.

Greater urgency could be obtained by recognising that regulation enjoys an overwhelmingly powerful sanction. In a regulated industry, if a cost cannot be directly related to a particular service provided to a particular customer, it is not proper to recover it from that customer. The licence condition which entitles BT to recover its costs entitles it only to the costs of providing the specific services against which such charges are levied. That is patently not the totality of BT's costs. Thus, there is no justification for charges levied for vague services such as access, water resources, network services, availability, capability, or capacity, and a regulatory blue pencil should exclude all items of this kind from a schedule of charges to customers. I have no doubt that the ability of regulated firms to establish chains of causality between costs and services would increase considerably once this became regulatory practice.

I believe that if these things are done, the variety of problems which arise from the apparent differences between average and incremental costs will, for all practical purposes, disappear. That enables the regulator to concentrate on the issues which ought properly to be of concern in this area. The starting point for all charging and tariff analysis is the incremental costs incurred by particular users of particular services, and that competition should be directed to those areas where the incremental costs of alternative provision are likely to be lower.

Three questions then arise. *First*, where are there economies of scale and scope, and what are the implications of their existence for the areas in which it is desirable and undesirable to promote competition? *Second*, what are the areas in which there is inefficiency, either as a result of excess capacity or of overmanning? *Third*, what is the degree of tariff averaging across the industry that is either desirable or necessary? To answer these questions would require several more papers.

6

REGULATING THE TRANSITION TO THE COMPETITIVE ELECTRICITY MARKET

Dr Dieter Helm
New College, Oxford

Introduction

THE ENERGY SECTOR HAS, by any reckoning, come through an extraordinary period of uncertainty and turmoil. Just three years since the restructuring and privatisation of the electricity industry, a major review of energy policy has been carried out, the coal industry has been radically cut down in size, and a new set of back-to-back contracts for the period 1993-98 has been put in place. The first supply review for the Regional Electricity Companies (RECs) which facilitates the new coal contracts has taken place. In the gas industry, the Monopolies and Mergers Commission (MMC) has pronounced on its review of British Gas, and effectively rejected the basis on which it was privatised. The Department of Trade and Industry has, in reaction, sanctioned a rapid fall in the domestic gas franchise.

At the time of writing, there is little evidence that the system is about to calm down. The Director General of OFFER is challenging the structure and pricing conduct of the two main fossil fuel generators, the future of the nuclear industry will be reviewed in 1994, the coal privatisation bill is before Parliament, and the major periodic review of the RECs' distribution business is under way. The franchise drop for the 100 KW–1 MW market is due in 1994. No other European energy market faces such upheaval and uncertainty.

Further out, more radical change is envisaged. The franchise drop in electricity in 1994 will be followed by abolition of franchises for both electricity and gas in 1998. At this date, the coal contracts will run out, probably spelling the end for the coal mining industry as a major force in the British energy market, and the levy supporting the nuclear industry expires. 1998, like 1993, is already destined to provide another contracting 'cliff-edge'.

These events have, of course, not all been the result of privatisation and the associated regulatory régime. A series of longer-term underlying fundamentals would, in any event, have necessitated considerable change.

This paper attempts to place regulatory performance and prospects within the context of the underlying fundamentals of the market. It is structured as follows. The next section identifies a number of stylised 'facts' underlying the energy sector into which the new regulatory régime has been introduced. The following section reviews regulatory policy in the transition to the competitive market largely with regard to electricity generation. The next section concentrates on the impact of regulation on prices. The final section then presents some suggestions about ways in which the current regulatory system could be modified to take account of the demands which may be placed upon it in the run up to 1998.

The Energy Fundamentals in the 1980s and Early 1990s

When historians come to review the performance of the energy sector since the change of government in 1979, there are two overwhelmingly important observations that will strike them. The first is that the oil price, having doubled in 1978-79 (following its quadrupling in 1972-73), collapsed. In real terms, oil is now cheaper than it was before the first oil shock. With that collapse came a corresponding fall in other primary fuel prices, most notably of coal and uranium. The second is that the developed economies – and especially Britain – performed worse and more erratically over the whole period since 1979 than they had even in the 1970s, and much worse than in the 1950s and 1960s. Consequently, demand has been much lower than could reasonably have been expected.

These two 'stylised facts' provide the context within which privatisation and the new regulatory régime were introduced. In electricity, a third feature characterised the industry – excess supply. Back in the 1970s, most of the decisions were taken which determined capacity in the electricity industry in the 1980s and early 1990s. In 1970, by which time most of the coal stations that now exist had been built or at least planned, the then Chairman of the CEGB, Sir Stanley Brown, in a lecture entitled *The next 25 years in the electricity supply industry*, extrapolated the past economic growth trends in output and energy demand to forecast that:

> '[M]y best guess is that over the next 25 years requirements for electricity are likely to increase at an average rate of around five per cent per annum cumulative, which would lead to peak demands of the order of 120,000 MW and unit sales of the order of 600,000 million kWh.' (S. Brown, 1970.)

In 1993/94, the forecast generating capacity including the Scottish link and Electricité de France is 59,600 MW, total consumption 271,000 kWh. At around half the forecast level, this leaves a comfortable 20·6 per cent capacity margin.[1]

It is now fashionable to deride the CEGB, and there have been a series of telling critiques of the CEGB's forecasting record and investment appraisal methods.[2] But, in transposing oneself back to 1970, it is not impossible to imagine making such a forecast, and this exposes a central economic characteristic of electricity supply: that long lead times mean that *ex post* investment 'mistakes' are likely, and that, given that they are likely, there is a need to establish a contractual relationship to share the risks with customers. Otherwise longer-term investments will be inadequately provided. Vertically integrated monopoly has been the traditional solution to the problem of credible commitments on the part of customers to the investors in long-term power projects and network transmission and distribution systems. Recent experience with Independent Power Producers (IPPs) and RECs illustrate this point, as we shall see below.

Plan for Coal and Nuclear Energy – the 1970s

The oil price shocks in the 1970s reinforced the rôle of coal and nuclear power within the British electricity system. *Plan for Coal* was in large measure a rational response to the first oil shock. British coal had become a valuable commodity, and it was not unreasonable to assume that, given the increasing dependence of the West on OPEC supplies and increased political militancy in the Middle East, OPEC would go

---

[1] Details of capacity forecasts are given in *Generation in the 1990s, the 1993 edition*, Oxford Economic Research Associates (OXERA) (1993a).

[2] See Robinson (1992) for a critique of the CEGB's forecasting record. See also Rees (1989) on the CEGB's investment behaviour.

on putting upward pressure on the price. The AGRs attracted the Labour Government, most notably Tony Benn, then Secretary of State for Energy.[3] Indeed, such was the certainty that nuclear would have a key rôle in a future high commodity price world that the Windscale Inquiry (HMSO, 1978) gave the go-ahead for the construction of THORP to reprocess spent fuel, on the grounds that uranium prices (and supplies) made reprocessing economic, and that a new generation of Fast Breeder Reactors (FBRs) would be needed, which would burn the plutonium.[4]

In 1979, when the Conservatives came to power, the electricity industry was overwhelmingly coal- and nuclear-based, and capacity and oil prices were at a peak. But almost immediately the recession began to bite. The period 1980-82 saw the introduction of the Medium Term Financial Strategy (MTFS) and, as the recession deepened, manufacturing output dropped by around 25 per cent – a phenomenon new to 20th-century British economic history. Although the recovery in the mid-1980s was sharp, aggregate growth over the period was sluggish, and by the end of the decade Britain was again in prolonged recession. In consequence, excess capacity dominated the entire period during which the new policies and regulation have operated. With the exception of Sizewell B, no significant construction of power stations took place throughout the 1980s, and Sizewell B itself is only now approaching commissioning.

Thus, the 1980s were overwhelmingly a decade of lower than expected oil prices, and lower than expected demand, serviced by an excess supply of predominantly coal-fired power stations, built under the opposite working assumptions. In consequence, in the 1980s, the investment question did not seriously arise. Energy policy could therefore be directed at the narrower question: how to minimise the operating costs of the existing system. The answer provided – competition and market forces – was broadly the right one for the 1980s. Unfortunately, as will be shown below, it was applied too late, and will have its most persuasive effects too late – that is, after 1998 when the franchise monopolies will be abolished. Furthermore, as we shall also

---

[3] See *Conflicts of Interest: Benn's Diaries, 1977-80* (1990, pp.260-64). The interpretation given there of the AGR decision is a controversial one. It should also be noted in this context that France and Germany also responded strategically with further nuclear commitments in this period. On this, see Price (1990), Ch.3.

[4] In this case, France, Japan and Russia followed suit. On the current THORP controversy, see Helm (1993b).

see below, despite the excess capacity, investment has been considerable.

Regulation and the Transition to the 'Competitive' Market in Electricity Generation

As the 1988 White Paper, *Privatising Electricity*, indicated, the primary objective was to provide for a competitive market in electricity generation and supply, and efficient regulation of the natural monopoly transmission and distribution systems. The merits of such a system had been set out as early as 1982 in a speech by the architect of this policy, the then Nigel Lawson.[5]

The most significant single feature of the new privatised régime was the splitting up of the CEGB between the potentially competitive generation activities and the national grid. The structure selected at the time was not perfect: the generation sector could then have been further disaggregated. However, given that the Conservative manifesto in 1987 committed the government to the inconsistent objectives of privatisation and a future programme of nuclear power, further restructuring of generation was impossible.[6] National Power was established as the dominant player, large enough, it was (erroneously) assumed, to bury the cost problems of nuclear, beyond those met by the fossil fuel levy. When the nuclear assets were finally withdrawn (to form Nuclear Electric), the residual of fossil fuel capacity in National Power still amounted to some 50 per cent of total capacity. The structural faults were not limited to generation: the failure fully to separate the National Grid Company (NGC) from the RECs was an additional error.

Transitionary Path to Competition

The new régime was set on a competitive transitionary path, to take almost a decade. Given the initial imperfections, the scale of the experiment, and the strategic importance of the electricity industry to the economy as a whole, such an evolutionary approach was a sensible one. The coal industry, inflated in size because of decisions made in the 1970s, was to be allowed to contract slowly with fixed price/fixed quantity contracts for the period 1990-93, ending safely after the last

---

[5] Lawson's speech is reprinted in Helm *et al.* (1989). For a discussion of the Lawson doctrine, see Helm (1993a).

[6] See Helm (1987).

possible date (1992) for the next General Election (when the UDM miners who had worked through the miners' strike could be released from political protection).[7] Once the initial coal contracts expired, the prospectuses indicated that generators would be free to purchase in a liberalised fuel market. The supply market was to be gradually exposed to competition in stages. Nuclear Electric was to preserve a special protected status until 1998, and the RECs were allowed a limited right to enter the generation market. In other words, a series of temporary barriers to competition would gradually unwind over the period.

This transitional period would, it was assumed, witness the adjustment of prices to their market levels. The government could not politically countenance the increase in prices at privatisation necessary fully to remunerate the full current cost value of the assets. Cecil Parkinson's 15 per cent pre-privatisation price hike was the maximum that politicians thought achievable. Nevertheless, the Department of Energy foresaw a gradual rise to the entry price, and this was encapsulated in the now famous Horton 4 scenario, widely used in attempting to place a value on the assets for financial instructions and, possibly, for Hanson.[8] This envisaged that prices would rise through the first three years to close to the entry level by 1993.

It was this transitionary process which OFFER was set up to oversee. The Director General of OFFER has had the management of this process as his major task, alongside the regulation of natural monopoly.[9] In 'promoting competition' he has, in effect, been promoting this transition. The task is probably the most demanding amongst the regulators and the Director General has approached the task of managing the transition in a number of distinct ways.[10] It is in this transitionary context that the performance of the regulatory régime

---

[7] See Helm (1993a) for a description of the political aspects of the privatisation, particularly the UDM protection after the miners' strike and Cecil Parkinson's pledge that prices would not go up as a result of privatisation.

[8] The government entered negotiations with Hanson over the sale of PowerGen, Hanson withdrew and PowerGen was then floated on the market along with National Power.

[9] For the Director General's views at the outset, see his statement, 17 October 1990. For his subsequent views see his speech, 15 October 1993.

[10] The Director General is associated with a particular theory of the competitive process, the Austrian School (see Hayek, 1948, for a classic statement). This theory is markedly different from conventional theories of competition, with distinct policy implications. A flavour of the Director General's broader views can be found in Littlechild (1981). On competition in electricity, see Littlechild (1993).

should be evaluated: in minimising costs and prices and providing the correct investment incentives.

The Regulator and the Generation Market

The Director General's primary focus has been on the generation market. The original transitionary process left the key strategic coal power stations in the hands of just two companies, National Power and PowerGen. Although it has come as an apparent surprise to some since then, it was a logical consequence of the initial privatisation that these two generators would have market power: given they had all the plant which sets prices at the margin, they set prices. As implied by the transitional process set up at privatisation, they will carry on doing so at least until 1998, unless the generation sector is radically dismembered before then, and the prospectuses abandoned.

It is, therefore, hardly surprising that the prices set by these two generators would be a focus of regular regulatory attention. In the first year after privatisation, the Large Industrial Customers (LICs) were protected by the LIC's scheme, and pool prices turned out to be some 25 per cent below expectations (Helm and Powell, 1991). They then rose as the LICs' protection fell away, and the contract cover changed, triggering the first OFFER pool prices inquiry. Such inquiries have now become virtually an annual event.[11]

These inquiries have provided a considerable insight into the Director General's view of the transitionary process and the promotion of competition. There is a possible conflict, at least in the short term, between the objectives of promoting competition, on the one hand, and looking after customers, on the other. In the transitionary period, customers are better off if prices are kept down. However, low prices make entry unattractive, especially when they are well below the entry level. The Director General therefore has had a problem to square: how to encourage entry, but limit prices below the level which makes entry economic. The solution he has chosen to adopt is ingenious.

As was already envisaged at privatisation, the primary vehicle for entry would be gas combined cycle gas turbines (CCGTs). Several projects were explicitly mentioned in the prospectuses, including Roosecote, where the contract had been signed. The problem that became apparent was that the private sector would not build such plants

---

[11] OFFER (1991, 1992, 1993).

on-spec, using the system marginal price (SMP) and the loss of land probability (LOLP) pool pricing mechanisms as the basis for rewarding investors for risk taking. On the contrary, no one (except National Power and PowerGen) was prepared to enter the market unless backed by a power purchase contract with a REC which assigned the price risk to the REC. Thus, the only source of 'entry' with which the Director General could promote competition were the RECs themselves, and they chose, in the face of regulatory encouragement, to integrate vertically into generation primarily through vertical contracts, and sometimes with equity stakes.[12]

The 'Dash for Gas'

The 'dash for gas' which followed had a significant regulatory element. Gas was the obvious fuel for new investment, but the hang-over of excess coal-fired capacity from the 1970s and 1980s meant that very little (if any) investment was actually needed.[13] The long recession, which was getting seriously underway at precisely the time of privatisation, undermined the capacity argument for the new CCGTs. Of course, they would in time be needed as the old coal assets wore out, but there was no immediate need to rush into gas in quite the numbers and scale which took place. The investment was largely in advance of need.

For the Director General, however, these new gas-fired power stations were a sign that competition was increasing. The number of 'competitors' was in effect equated to the degree of competition. Such a view clearly did not convince everyone, especially the House of Commons Select Committee on Energy (see the report, HMSO, 1992). The Director General investigated whether the RECs had in fact met their economic purchasing obligation in their licences (condition 5) in line with his preferred broad interpretation set out at the time of privatisation.[14] OFFER's *Review of Economic Purchasing* (published in

---

[12] The RECs were limited through their licences in vertically integrating through ownership to a quota. However, most of the features of ownership can be replicated through contracts, so the constraint has in practice provided only a weak obstacle.

[13] It has been argued that the requirement to limit emissions of sulphur dioxide gave a clear rationale for gas investment. Whilst new gas CCGTs may have provided a cheaper option to the fitting of Flue Gas Desulphurisers on old coal plant, the government in the event required a programme of FGD investments.

[14] The report of the Select Committee (1992) on the *Consequences of Electricity Privatisation* explicitly addressed this issue.

two reports, December 1992, February 1993) provided a comparison of prices rather than costs. In it, the Director General stated that no REC went to full open tender (para.64, December 1992). Indeed, the two reports were at great pains to stress that the contracting strategies of the RECs were based on a desire to diversify away from National Power and PowerGen rather than on narrow price comparisons. (If this was a sufficient justification in fulfilment of condition 5, then there was strictly no need to compare IPPs with generator prices at all.)

The absence of a requirement to tender competitively is extremely hard to reconcile with the Director General's preference for competitive solutions: at minimum, the tendering of the contract volume should have been required to meet the licence condition. It is also worth noting that the Director General's views on economic purchasing seem at some variance with those given by the last Secretary of State for Energy, John Wakeham, who told the Select Committee on Energy that

> 'The regional electricity companies have an obligation for economic purchasing. If they have got – I put it absolutely crudely so there is no doubt about it – an interest in a gas-fired power station which gives to them electricity which is more expensive than the electricity they can buy from another source, in my judgement they are in breach of their licence condition. They have to buy the cheapest electricity in the market.'[15]

The Secretary of State thus considered the matter to be about price, not diversification strategy, and given that comparative contracts from PowerGen and National Power were, as the Director General's reports recognise, not actively pursued, the two interpretations have markedly different consequences. If the RECs had not – through competitive tendering – sought 'the cheapest electricity in the market', it was reasonable to argue that they had not met the condition.

The reality, of course, is that the Director General's position would, in practice, probably have been untenable had he found against the REC-IPP contracts: his apparent implicit objective of maximising the number of competitors would have been abruptly undermined, and some RECs might have questioned the comfort they thought they had got in their earlier discussions with him. The *Review of Economic Purchasing* was, in many respects, an analysis looking to provide a particular answer.

---

[15] Select Committee on Energy (1992), Vol.1, para.56.

Promotion of CCGTs

The strategy of promoting competition through the promotion of CCGTs has been successful to the extent that it has increased the number of non-National Power/PowerGen stations. There are many more in prospect, but their economics are increasingly uncertain. Thus, in the search for more entrants, the Director General has now turned his attention to the coal stations which are being closed as a result of physical depreciation, the surge in gas and the increase in output from Nuclear Electric. The Director General appears to view these stations as another source of competition: if only they could be bought up by 'independents' there would be a higher number of competitors. The Director General, however, clearly ran into considerable opposition when considering his options.[16] An independent assessment was required via a licence amendment of closure decisions rather than the full requirement to sell.

There are several difficulties associated with this source of increasing competition. The first is that the two fossil fuel generators have been 'persuaded' by the Government to take considerably more coal for the five-year period 1993-98 than they would have done had the original transition been adhered to. Indeed, on the assumption that the liberalised fuel purchasing would apply from March 1993, they even invested in import terminals. The rational strategy, given the coal stocks, would have been to buy no coal at all from British Coal after March 1993 for some months to take down the stocks first, and then enter into short-term, variable supply contracts. The failure to liberalise was a significant blow to the transition process. If existing coal stations are taken over by 'competitors' free to buy coal at lower prices than those forced upon the generators, the loss of market share would introduce a very significant economic loss to National Power and PowerGen. Worse still, the potential owners of the old stations might write must-take coal contracts themselves, and hence run *less efficient* plant at *base load*, thereby breaching the merit order of plant. Finally, by taking plant out of mid-merit into base load, such changes might actually *increase* the market power of the two fossil-fuel generators, since their remaining plant might have even more influence over price.

In sum, the Director General has clearly been frustrated by the market power bequeathed to the generators at privatisation. His consistent efforts to increase competition have been focussed on the RECs-IPPs

---

[16] This is recognised in OFFER Press Release, 20 April 1993.

and now on coal plant for closure. However, in a period of excess supply, such regulatory interventions in the generation market may have the effect of advancing investment ahead of necessity, causing more rapid closures for the coal industry, and even out-of-merit bidding. Getting the timing wrong is not a technicality: there are real economic costs associated with it. These are the additional costs customers are paying now for the promised benefits from the 'competition' in the future.

Assessing the Consequences of the Drive for Competition

When our historian, with whom we began, looks back at the 1990s, he will observe two clear trends: the speed with which gas came into the market, and the speed with which the coal industry collapsed. It is, however, reasonable to ask whether these trends really matter. Performance should not be judged against some idealised perfect hindsight, but rather against the more practical context in which decisions have been made.

The first method of assessment is to compare the current performance with that of the regulatory system it replaced. Would the CEGB have done any better under civil servant and ministerial regulation? There are few reasons for thinking it would. Indeed, instead of the dash-for-gas, Lord Marshall and John Baker, at the CEGB, would probably have pushed on with a new programme of PWR reactors. We might have had a 'dash-for-nuclear': up to 10 were discussed in the mid-1980s, to follow on from Sizewell B. Planning permission for Hinkley C was actually achieved. Mrs Thatcher was an ardent supporter, and this was reflected in the 1987 Conservative manifesto. These reactors would have come on later, in that they do not have the attractive feature of rapid construction which CCGTs have displayed. However, their economic characteristics are far from attractive, and the record of the CEGB in managing nuclear construction is not good. Only the fiscal priorities of the Treasury might have saved the industry from this outcome in the state sector.[17]

However, not everything the CEGB did was badly planned or executed. The merit order would have been maintained, and closures would probably have been carried out in a manner which gave more order to the market. The fate of the coal industry would not have been

---

[17] In this context, it is interesting to note that Nuclear Electric, which has taken over the CEGB's nuclear assets, is actively promoting Sizewell C twin-PWR and a further family of PWRs thereafter.

tied to the 1993 deadline, and its run-down would probably have been more gradual.

Impact on Prices and Customers

The second way of approaching the assessment of performance is to consider the impact on customers, and hence the behaviour of prices. To what extent has regulation been effective in the domain of pricing?

There can be little doubt that competitive pressures and RPI-X price caps have had very great beneficial effects on operating costs. The over-manning which characterised the CEGB has been sharply eroded. The RECs, under RPI-X price caps, can maximise profits by minimising costs. But the over-riding important feature of the period has been the fall in primary fuel prices: the prices of coal, oil, gas and uranium have continued to fall throughout the period since privatisation. Therefore, it would be rather surprising if prices had not fallen. The issue is not *whether* prices have fallen, but rather *by how much*.

In this context, the impact of regulation deserves very close scrutiny. In the chain of costs from coal through to the final customer, most of the basic elements have been fixed outside the competitive market, by government and regulators. The price of coal has been determined by politically-driven contracts, first for 1990-93 and then for 1993-98. The generators' prices to the RECs were largely fixed in the period 1990-93 through the vesting contracts-for-differences, and then again through back-to-back contracts with the new coal contracts. The prices charged by the National Grid Company (NGC) have been fixed under its price cap, which has been reviewed once. RECs' supply and distribution prices are also covered by price caps (though for supply only in the franchise market).

There can be little doubt that, since privatisation, prices in all stages of this chain have not fallen as fast as costs. But it is important to interpret this result carefully: we must not assume that prices were 'right' at privatisation. Indeed, as commented on above, quite the contrary was the case – prices were not sufficient to reward the current cost value of the assets of the generators and many of the RECs.[18]

Much then of the performance of prices has been determined outside the scope of competition. Some aspects of pricing have, however,

---

[18] This aspect of the asset valuations has been brought to the fore in the MMC (1993) gas inquiry. As in US regulation, rates of return and asset valuations are taking an increasingly important rôle in setting RPI-X, further eroding the differences between the two approaches which were stressed at privatisation.

fallen within the scope of the Director General. In particular, the Director General has intervened over pool prices on a number of occasions and he has reset some price caps. He has also *not* used his powers to intervene between price cap reviews, despite the very considerable profits which have been earned by the RECs.[19]

Pool Prices

I will take each of these in turn. On pool prices, the Director General has, as noted above, compiled a number of reports. His statements have been perplexing. Using a relatively crude top-down approach, he appeared to claim that National Power and PowerGen were pricing *below* their avoidable costs. He gave an example of his calculations from National Power's accounts. Pool prices then rose to a level broadly consistent with the Director General's definition. He subsequently revised his view, chose another bottom-up definition of avoidable costs, and concluded that prices were *above* this level. (He had also stated, as we noted above, that the CCGT prices – the entry prices – met the economic purchasing obligation of the RECs. These were, at the time, *above* the pool prices.)

During 1993 and 1994 the Director General has been deliberating on these matters further, in reaching his decision on whether to refer the generators to the MMC. The Director General's decision has been complicated by the context of the pricing behaviour of National Power and PowerGen. As indicated above, this should include the REC-IPP contracts (and the associated lack of competitive bidding for them), the Director General's various definitions of avoidable costs, the Horton 4 forecasts and, of course, the influence of the policy-induced artificial coal contracts.

Price Cap Reviews

Turning to the price cap reviews, and the absence of intervention between periodic review, the Director General has regarded the essence of such 'contracts' as fixed-price for a fixed-period, in order to maximise efficiency incentives.[20] Unlike many of the other regulators,

---

[19] It is in this context of high returns that the good relations between the companies and the regulator in the electricity industry which the Director General comments on in his Press Release, 20 April 1993, should be interpreted.

[20] He was the author of the RPI-X rule for BT: see HMSO (1983). See also Beesley and Littlechild (1989).

he has doggedly stuck to his principles, as the recession bit deeply and as the profits and returns to REC shareholders have greatly increased.

The argument against intervention is that it removes the incentive to drive down costs and drives up the cost of capital for new investment. In the water industry, where investment is significant, intervention has nevertheless become an almost annual event. But, in the case of the RECs, such an investment argument is much harder to make: the distribution systems are very mature. Investment requirements are correspondingly small. Furthermore, it is very hard to imagine that, if the Director General had lowered prices during the first period, RECs would have given up their drive to operating efficiency. Quite the contrary: in order to satisfy their shareholders they – like many recession-hit firms – would respond to a price cut by redoubling their efforts. In a competitive market, prices vary and price shocks are the norm. Prices are not fixed for neat five-year periods. If anything, the failure to intervene has allowed a more leisurely approach to cost-cutting, and permitted some strategic behaviour around the approach to the periodic distribution review.[21]

The formulae that have been reset are for NGC and the supply businesses of the RECs. On the former, so little information about the assumptions and processes by which the X factor was arrived at has been revealed that it is very hard to form any judgement.[22] British regulators give the scantest of reasons for their decisions, making assessment and challenge by third parties (like customers) practically impossible.

On the supply price cap, more has leaked out about the process, though most evidence is anecdotal. The outcome was within a small plausible range, given that margins on the RECs' supply franchise business are, in any event, very tight and high margins are necessary to attract new competitors.

Non-Intervention Stance

The real importance of the supply price cap review relates to the pass through of coal costs. At the time of the renegotiation of the coal contracts, which began before the 1992 General Election and carried on

---

[21] The Director General's powers of direct intervention are limited. However, his indirect powers are considerable: he could have threatened an MMC reference, and this would almost certainly have led to compliance.

[22] See OFFER statement, 7 July 1992.

throughout 1992 and into early 1993, it was widely recognised that a full market solution for fuel purchase along the lines of the original transition plan would have led to a collapse of the coal industry over a very short period. However, the additional costs of British Coal could only be borne by the market if someone picked up the cost. The only serious candidate (since the Treasury would not pay) was the RECs' franchise customer base. However, the price cap for the RECs' supply business was to be reviewed for resetting in mid-1993 – after the recontracting deadline for coal. Therefore, the prospect of a new deal for coal depended on the Director General allowing the costs to be passed through to final customers (Helm, 1992). This he resolutely refused to do: higher coal costs meant higher prices to final customers and new back-to-back coal contracts reduced the scope for competition in the electricity market.

The political pressures during the coal crisis were obviously enormous. In January 1993, the Director General set out his views to the Government in a letter (dated 11 January). In it, he effectively conceded the cost-pass-through for the coal contracts as a price he would accept if the franchise drop in 1994 was allowed to go ahead (Helm, 1993a). It was a turning point, a piece of masterly political manoeuvre. Customers would therefore pay the higher coal costs, but the transition to supply competition was preserved.

In maintaining the path to franchise deregulation, the Director General has been very consistent. Competition, he argues, is worth paying for. Just as he had argued that customers will, in the longer run, benefit from the non-interference in price caps now by having more efficient companies later, so customers should pay now for the benefits that supply competition is assumed to bring.

Mixed Record

All in all, the record on prices has been a mixed one. Prices could undoubtedly have been lower now had the Director General chosen to intervene. When the British record is compared with other European countries, British prices have not fallen relative to the main competitor countries. In that section of the market where international competitiveness matters most (the LICs), they have risen, and in some cases steeply. There is, then, little evidence to show that customers are – given the low demand, excess capacity and the collapse of fuel prices (our stylised facts) – much better off as a result of the operation of the new system. Some, but by no means all, of this performance falls within the ambit of the explicit and implicit powers of the Director

General. Given the claims that have been made for the superiority of the British system over every other system of utility regulation in Europe and that in the USA, it is very surprising that after three years there is so little to show in the electricity market.

Looking Forward: The Future of the Transition and the Prospects for 1998

A central theme of this paper has been that the effective design of regulation depends upon the underlying fundamentals: there is no unique 'best' regulatory system, independent of the context within which it operates.

The context for the rest of the decade is largely focussed on preparations for the events scheduled for 1998. On 31 March 1998, the coal contracts will end along with the contracts-for-difference between the generators and the RECs. All domestic electricity and gas franchises will also end as the transition is completed. The nuclear levy also expires.

There is much debate and uncertainty about precisely how this final stage of the transition will come about, and considerable debate about its consequences. It will greatly depend upon the context. Unlike the 1980s and early 1990s, that context will be increasingly dominated by investment towards and beyond the turn of the century. Most coal stations will be around 30 years old by 2000, and the Magnoxes will be closed or closing. The key issue then will be whether the coal stations are refurbished, gas CCGTs take the dominant share of the market or more PWRs are built (and, of course, the extent of energy efficiency). To consider these issues, we need to begin where we started – with the oil price.

The prediction of oil prices is a hazardous business. The degree of uncertainty is very great, because the determination of the price is in large measure independent, at least in the short run, of fundamentals as supplies are located predominantly in politically sensitive areas. From the point of view of the electricity system, however, the issue is not whether a particular forecast is correct. Rather the question is: If oil prices rose significantly in the second half of the decade, how would the system cope?

A rise in oil prices would have serious consequences. In effect, the British electricity system would have run down its coal industry just as it became valuable. Having kept output up in the expectation of high oil prices in the 1970s and for political reasons in the 1980s, it would now be collapsed down to a residual when oil prices were high.[23] Similarly, the moratorium on the building of nuclear power plants beyond Sizewell B in the 1980s and 1990s would mean that the share of nuclear power would decline, when its economic value was increasing.

Government Forecasting 'Not Very Good'

The lesson from the 1970s is that governments are not very good at predicting, and that too great an emphasis on point predictions may have significant costs. The task of energy policy in this context is to ensure that appropriate insurance is taken. That does not mean giving the go-ahead to a family of PWRs. But it also does not mean relying entirely on the market. Unfashionable as it may be to point out, the private sector's record in this area is not much better than that of the public sector. Indeed, it was investment failures which provided one motivation for nationalisation.

The current system is neither planned nor strictly market-driven. Capacity decisions have been determined by a combination of regulatory bias and political action. New gas capacity depends on vertically integrated contracts with the RECs, of between 10 and 15 years. As argued above, these have not been subjected to a market test. Rather they have artificially displaced coal stations. In this regard, the market is not competitive enough. A case can be argued that compulsory market testing should be applied – including coal-based bids from the existing generators.

The life of existing coal stations is not entirely market-determined either: the artificial contracts now in place create an economic incentive on the fossil fuel generators to burn the excess volume. If fuel purchase is driven by political considerations, then it will affect asset lives. Furthermore, a requirement to fit FGDs would effectively close much of the remaining coal stations.

Other investments are much more explicitly biased by government. Nuclear investment has never had much to do with competition and market forces, and it is very unlikely that any new investment in PWRs would be market-led. Investments in renewables are artificially subsidised through part of the levy. Finally, investments in energy demand reduction are subsidised through the Energy Efficiency Trust.

---

[23] See OXERA (1993b), *Coal in the UK: Prospects for the Industry*, for an analysis of the likely scale of the coal industry in 1998. This is to be compared with the estimates in the Government's White Paper (Department of Trade and Industry, 1993)

Regulatory Bias and Government Intervention in Investment

Thus, far from being market-driven, determined by competitive forces, investment in the electricity industry is in practice determined in large measure by a combination of regulatory bias to increase the number of competitors and government intervention. There is very little overall coherence, with the result that a significant *ad hoc* element is introduced.

There are two possible solutions to this investment problem in the run up to 1998 and beyond. The *first* – the Director General's preference – is seriously to pursue the market solution – that is, to implement the vision of a free market in electricity which Nigel Lawson first advocated. To the purists, this has a lot of attractions. The *second* is to be pragmatic – to admit that, whether one approves or not, governments will always interfere in investment decisions, that private markets as well as governments are prone to failure, and that the electricity market is unlikely ever to approximate the textbook model of competitive markets. In this second-best world, the issue is not simply to appeal to the doctrine of competition, but rather how to create a framework within which the maximum benefits can be reached from the operation of market forces in the framework of government policy, set in a well-defined and consistent fashion.

This second route is, of course, far from simple and straightforward. To be workable, it needs to build on the strengths of the current system, to be evolutionary rather than revolutionary. This is not the place to outline such an alternative scheme in detail. Elsewhere I have indicated that it should contain a number of elements, based upon the idea of capacity auctions supported by an Energy Agency.[24]

On the second view, whether the current system of regulation is sustainable will therefore depend upon the development of a coherent framework of energy policy within which market forces are given the maximum extent consistent with that framework. To continue down the present road – the transition – will not be disastrous if the current assumptions about the fundamentals are realised (that oil prices will stay low and economic growth will be sluggish) and therefore the investment problem is postponed.

However, as I have tried to illustrate in this paper, the energy problems of the 1980s and early 1990s have been very much the result of a set of assumptions which turned out to be the opposite of the

---

[24] See Helm (1992).

outturn (that demand would grow throughout the period and that oil prices would be high). If current assumptions turn out to be wrong – if oil prices shoot up and growth resumes – then Britain may well find that, precisely when it needs its coal (and perhaps nuclear too), its electricity system and associated regulation have significantly closed off these options. Because the government and the CEGB were not good predictors in the past does not prove that the private sector is immune from investment 'mistakes'. And because many would wish the government not to interfere does not mean that it will not. Therefore, I conclude by urging a practical and pragmatic way forward, rather than simple adherence to the doctrine of competition.

BIBLIOGRAPHY

Beesley, M. E., and S. Littlechild (1989): 'The Regulation of Privatised Monopolies in the United Kingdom', *Rand Journal*, Vol.20, pp.454-72.

Benn, T. (1990): *Conflicts of Interest: Diaries 1977-80*, London: Arrow Books.

Brown, S. (1970): *The Next 25 Years in the Electricity Supply Industry*, London: CEGB.

Department of Energy (1988): *Privatising Electricity*, Cm.322, London: HMSO.

Department of Trade and Industry (1993): *The Prospects for Coal: Conclusions at the Government's Coal Review*, Cm.2235, March.

Hayek, F.A. (1948): *Individualism and Economic Order*, Chicago: University of Chicago Press.

Helm, D.R. (1987): 'Nuclear Power and the Privatisation of Electricity Generation', *Fiscal Studies*, Vol.8, pp.69-73.

Helm, D.R., J.A. Kay and D. Thompson (eds.) (1989): *The Market for Energy*, Oxford University Press.

Helm, D.R., and A. Powell, (1991): 'Pool Prices, Contracts & Regulation in the British Electricity Supply Industry', *Fiscal Studies*, Vol.13 (1).

Helm, D.R. (1992): Minutes of Evidence to the House of Commons Trade and Industry Committee Enquiry, *British Energy Policy and the Market for Coal*, HC 237-iii, London: HMSO, November, pp.55-60.

Helm, D.R. (1993a): 'Energy Policy and Market Doctrine', *Political Quarterly*, pp.410-19.

Helm, D.R. (1993b): 'The Economics of THORP', *Energy Utilities*, November.

House of Commons Select Committee on Energy (1992): *Consequences of Electricity Privatisation*, London: HMSO.

House of Commons Select Committee on Trade and Industry (1993): *British Energy Policy and the Market for Coal* (First Report, 1992/93), HC237, London: HMSO.

HMSO (1978): *The Windscale Inquiry*, Report by Hon Mr Justice Parker, London: HMSO.

HMSO (1983): *Regulation of British Telecommunications' Profitability*, London: HMSO.

Lawson, N. (1982): Speech on Energy Policy, in Helm *et al.* (1989).

Littlechild, S.C. (1981): 'Ten Steps to Denationalistion', *Economic Affairs*, Vol.2, October, pp.11-19.

Littlechild, S.C. (1993): 'New Developments in Electricity Regulation', in M. E. Bcesley (ed.), *Major Issues in Regulation*, IEA Readings No.40, London: IEA/LBS.

MMC (1993): *Gas and British Gas plc*, Cm.2316, London: HMSO.

OFFER (1990): 'The Regulatory System and the Duties of the DGES', Statement by the Director General, 17 October.

OFFER (1991): *Report on Pool Price Inquiry*.

OFFER (1992): *Review of Pool Prices*.

OFFER (1992): 'Future Control on National Grid Company Prices', Statement by the Director General, 7 July.

OFFER (1992): *Review of Economic Purchasing*, December.

OFFER (1993): *Pool Price Statement*.

OFFER (1993): Letter to the Rt Hon T. Eggar MP by the Director General, 1 November.

OFFER (1993): *Review of Economic Purchasing*, Further Statements, February.

OFFER (1993): 'Debate on Regulatory Framework Should be Better Informed', Press Release, 20 March.

OFFER (1993): 'The Development of Competition in Electricity Supply', Speech at the Pool 100kW Seminar, 15 October.

OXERA (1993a): *Generation in the 1990s: the 1993 Edition*, Oxford.

OXERA (1993b): *Coal in the UK: Prospects for the Industry*, Oxford.

Price, T. (1990): *Political Electricity: What Future for Nuclear Energy?*, Oxford University Press.

Rees, R. (1989): 'Modelling Public Enterprise Performance', in Helm *et al.* (eds.) (1989).

Robinson, C. (1992): 'The Demand for Electricity: A Critical Analysis of Producer Forecasts', in D. Hawdon (ed.), *Energy Demand: Evidence and Expectations*, Guildford: Surrey University Press.

CHAIRMAN'S COMMENTS

Professor Stephen Littlechild
OFFER

$\mathbf{D}$IETER'S PAPER WAS A MASTERLY SURVEY of not only the present but also of the history of the electricity industry, and in particular the development of regulatory policy.

Though he is very encouraging in a number of respects, I did detect a *soupçon* of concern in one or two areas. One concern is economic purchasing, and whether there has been an excessive dash for gas. He draws attention to an apparent difference between the view that Lord Wakeham expressed, which in a nutshell was that only price counts; and the view that I expressed, which is that one cannot look at price alone: a variety of other considerations had to be taken into account. If one looks simply at the Act, there is no doubt that it, and, following it, the licence, make explicit provision for a variety of other considerations to be taken into account, such as diversity of supply.

The apparent difference between Lord Wakeham and me is not necessarily as great as might appear if one puts in the phrase 'over the relevant period' into his statement. In other words, if one looks not just at one year, but at a period of years, it becomes more relevant to take into account the path of prices. And what the RECs argued, quite strongly, was that it was necessary and desirable to bring in alternative forms of competition to the existing generators in the industry. That would have beneficial effects on the efficiency of the existing generators and on the prices RECs paid, and consequently what customers paid. My examination of prices found that the prices that the RECs had signed for the IPPs compared well with the alternatives available, so it did not seem to me that there was a serious conflict of view there.

Dieter advocates tendering. In general, tendering has much to commend it, but I am not sure that it would have made a significant difference in this case. If the purpose of contracting out with an independent power producer was to bring in more competition, that could have been a worthwhile strategy in its own right. It is not clear to me how getting tenders from the incumbent generators to supply the same electricity would serve the purpose.

Price Controls on RECs

Dieter also has reservations about whether or not I should have intervened to change and tighten the price controls on the regional electricity companies' distribution businesses because high profits were being earned there. There is no doubt that high profits were and are being earned there, certainly higher than were expected at the time the price contracts were set. I also accept, indeed I have never argued otherwise, that if one were to change them, there would be reductions in prices to customers. I agree that it is doubtful if that would have an adverse effect on the cutting of costs in the short term. But one has to look further. Stepping in to intervene here would have had a number of implications. At a relatively early stage one would have been calling in to question the whole regulatory régime, and in particular an expectation that had been set up at the time of Vesting. That would have had adverse implications in the electricity industry reaching beyond the regional electricity companies.

Even if one looks only at the regional electricity companies themselves, there would have been adverse effects. *First*, the cost of capital would have increased because investors would now be saying that this is a much more uncertain regulatory régime than they expected, and that they needed a higher return to compensate them. We made some rough calculations which suggested that the present value of those adverse effects, even for a small increase in the cost of capital, outweighed the benefit from reducing prices in the short term.

Second, stepping in would set up an expectation that if things turned out differently than expected when the price control was set, the price control would be re-opened. Any regulated company could then come along and say 'my costs are higher than I expected, therefore I need a price increase'. What is sauce for the goose is sauce for the gander. If costs were lower than expected, that also could be regarded as a reason for re-opening the issue. If you did not resist the one call, you cannot resist the other. You are then increasingly into a situation where you look at frequent intervals, perhaps even annual intervals, at what costs have been, what they are likely to be. You could well be into a situation where you are changing prices almost year by year. To distinguish between that and a normal cost pass-through arrangement seems very difficult. The adverse incentive effects could well be very significant.

Rôle of Government in Investment Planning

The third area that I would comment on briefly, to try to elucidate Dieter's thinking a little more, is on the rôle of government planning he envisages. Now, in the text rather than in his talk, he emphasises that whereas the present arrangements may conceivably be defended as appropriate during a time of low demand, excess capacity and low oil prices, they are much more questionable at a time of high demand and a high oil price. And he questions whether the investment programme that has been seen over the past few years is the appropriate one for such a future.

He has given us one scenario but one has to look at a whole range of scenarios. The investment programmes that generators, or other companies for that matter, engage in have to take into account a variety of possible futures. One of them would be Dieter's, but there would be others, involving, for example, more severe environmental constraints. It is not clear to me that when you look at that broad range of scenarios, and the probabilities of each of them happening, the investment programme that has actually taken place would be less efficient than an alternative that Dieter has in mind. Can one argue that the market, broadly speaking, has made mistakes when taking into account the possible futures and their likelihood?

Why is it, then, that Dieter is arguing a need for more planning and central direction? He paints as quite distinct alternatives either a rather doctrinaire favouring of competition, or a realistic acceptance of the fact that governments will tend to intervene. Well, we all accept that governments, from time to time, do indeed wish to intervene and in any democratic society there will always be political pressures for them to do so. That is not really an issue. The question is: How much scope do you allow for it? And, indeed, to what extent do you encourage or discourage it? Do you look for a system which, on the whole, tries to maximise the scope for markets and competition to take decisions and allocate resources, tending to limit the scope for government intervention? Or do you look for a system which tends to minimise the scope for markets and competition, and tends to maximise the scope for government?

I think Dieter argues for a system which gives greater facility for governments to intervene and indeed invites them to do so. The sort of suggestions that he has made elsewhere, and to which he refers briefly in his paper, for example, of options for amounts of capacity to be specified by an energy agency, obviously give government a very great deal of control indeed over the development of the industry. I am not clear why Dieter thinks this would be beneficial. If he is arguing that the market makes mistakes and the Government Planning Agency can do better, he has not yet established his case. All the evidence is, I think, that government planning tends to lead to much higher costs and much larger-scale mistakes.

7

THE REGULATION OF BRITAIN'S PRIVATISED RAILWAYS

Stephen Glaister
The London School of Economics

THE DETAILS OF THE PROPOSALS presently before Parliament are not well known and so I thought it would be useful to take time to set them out. I will then identify some of the issues which emerge for the attention of the Regulator. I fear that I will be able to do little more than make a catalogue of unanswered questions. A great deal of work has already been done, but there is more to be done on many of the issues before a view can be made public. In some cases firm proposals will have to come from others before the Regulator can respond.

I am sure that some more apposite phrase than 'railway privatisation' would have come into use were it not for the irresistible temptation to draw an analogy with the privatisations that have gone before. The temptation may have been increased by the similarities of the Railways Bill to the other Acts – although my legally expert friends tell me that there are significant differences. I conclude the paper by discussing the many ways in which this 'privatisation' is different from the previous ones and I note some of the tensions that are created by the present proposals.

I will say little about the wider political economy of the subject: that is discussed in the IEA paper by Tony Travers and me, published by the IEA in June 1993.[1]

First, let me make it clear that the Railway regulator has not been appointed. Mr John Swift QC holds the position of Special Advisor to the Secretary of State, until Royal Assent.[2] He is in the process of setting up an 'expeditionary' office, in the refurbished Prudential

---

[1] *New Directions for British Railways? The Political Economy of Privatisation and Regulation*, Current Controversies No.5, London: Institute of Economic Affairs, 1993.

[2] Postscript: Mr Swift was duly appointed as Regulator in November 1993.

building in Holborn. Although I am giving him some assistance on a part-time basis, I am speaking entirely on my own behalf and not representing him, or the Department of Transport.

I will not be saying anything further on the subject of safety. All parties recognise the importance of the topic and that it has to be got 'right'. In view of the potential for safety-based regulation to interact – and interfere – with economic regulation, the Regulator's interest will obviously extend beyond the 'mechanics' of safety assurance. Some of the risks to be avoided are the creation of unnecessary barriers to entry and slow-moving safety approval processes.

The Policy Context

A statement of what the railways policy is intended to achieve is set out in the White Paper:

> 'The Government is determined to see better use made of the railways, greater responsiveness to the customer, and a higher quality of service and better value for money for the public who travel by rail' (White Paper, 1992, para.1).

In other documents the Government has made statements like 'The Government will continue to ensure that [there are] sufficient funds to support socially necessary services' (*Gaining Access...*, para 6.18), but there can be no doubt that the Government would be pleased if the policy were able to achieve this whilst reducing state support to the industry, currently of the order of £1 billion per annum – in other words, a lighter burden for the tax-payer as well as better value for money for the public who travel by rail.

Increasing competition is seen as the major strategic weapon in achieving the objectives. There are two distinct strands to this. *First*, there is competition amongst train operators for the passenger and freight markets. *Second*, there is competition in the provision of the goods and services required by Railtrack. The first of these has received most public attention but, as I shall argue, the second is at least as important.

Statement of the New Proposals

o *Railtrack*: will stay within the public sector in the short term. It will be a 'GoCo', a company under the provisions of the Companies Act 1985 with all the issued shares held by the Secretary of State. This will be a similar arrangement to that which applies to London Buses Ltd and London Underground Ltd., which are technically subsidiaries of London Regional Transport under the Companies Act.

Railtrack will operate, maintain and invest in the fixed infrastructure, principally track and signalling. It will be responsible for defining train paths and timetabling them.

There has been no public announcement of the details of Railtrack's objectives but the White Paper (para.23) states:

> 'The Government believes that revenue subsidies should be targeted directly to the provision of services. Railtrack will not therefore be subsidised (although it will be eligible for capital grants in certain circumstances...) and will be expected to make a return on its assets and to charge operators for the use of its track.'

The Secretary of State will retain the power to give capital grants direct to Railtrack if justified on cost/benefit grounds.

Whilst Railtrack remains within the public sector it will be caught within the normal process of three-year public expenditure planning with all that implies. Access to funds will be constrained by the External Financing Limits, rates of return will be laid down, investment projects will be subject to scrutiny and the other attributes of public sector will remain.

In the early stages the Franchising Director will specify something close to the existing timetable for Railtrack to operate. Over time it is envisaged that the varying pressures from the different markets to which Railtrack sells its capacity will lead to changes.

Arguably the most important change in the provision of infrastructure will follow from the fact that Railtrack will 'buy in' most of its services under competition (infrastructure maintenance, signalling repairs, investment, etc.) initially from British Rail and, over time, from the private sector as these activities are transferred from BR ownership.

○ *The Franchising Director*: will define services, singly or in bundles, which will be offered to independent train operators under competitive tender. The successful bid may be positive or negative. The contract bid for will specify the services to be offered and the Franchising Director will have 'booked' the appropriate train paths with Railtrack in advance on known terms.

The Government intends that eventually it will pass all of the financial support for the railways through the Franchising Director with the exception of certain capital grants. It will be the Franchising Director's responsibility to determine the level of subsidy required to maintain each service.

The Franchising Director will be set objectives by and be answerable to the Secretary of State who will set a budget. These objectives are not explicitly set out in the Bill, apart from a duty to achieve them economically and efficiently.

The Franchising Director will be, to all intents and purposes, in a similar position to a nationalised industry.

o *British Rail Operations and Infrastructure Services*: will continue for a period – possibly for several years – while services are progressively franchised and infrastructure is transferred. The Government will continue to exercise the same régime of normal public sector scrutiny as now. Operations will be separate from Railtrack and it will have a new and separate management structure. British Rail Infrastructure Services will be created as a holding company initially employing over 40,000 people. This will create new markets in infrastructure services and sell its trading activities to the private sector.

o *The Government*: will set objectives and budgets. It can pay subsidy under several different headings. It can also intervene directly as it increasingly does with the present nationalised industries. Interestingly, the Government will be Railtrack's shareholder and also the funder of Railtrack's main customer, the Franchising Director.

Several production activities which are currently subject to government objectives by virtue of being within British Railways, will escape from them: for instance, franchised train operations, vehicle leasing, track engineering.

o *The Regulator*: is to be established as an independent entity. He will issue licences to operators (or grant exemptions to the need to be licensed). He will resolve disputes, prevent anti-competitive practices in the setting of charges and the making of agreements between the active parties.

A significant proportion of his power resides in the fact that he has to approve all access agreements, and this will be a continuing and frequent process.

He will oversee the agreements giving train service operators access to infrastructure, the agreements between the franchised service operators and the Franchising Director, and the operation of fares control formulae which may be set as licence conditions on operators. He will approve the charging régime set by Railtrack for the use of the infrastructure.

The Regulator will also deal with up to 10 Rail Users' Consultative Committees and a Central Rail Users' Committee. He will receive proposals from the Franchising Director for service closures and consider them, possibly in the forum of a public inquiry. If the Regulator decides on closure, appeals may be made to the Secretary of State who will have a power to pay direct subsidy to forestall closure.

The Specific Functions and Duties of the Regulator

Control will be exercised by a system of licences and contractual agreements. These will spell out the rights and obligations and penalties for non-compliance of the various parties.

There will be franchise agreements between the Franchising Director and the franchised passenger train operating companies. The arrangements for through ticketing and concessionary fares will be enforced through them. The Regulator has no direct concern with franchise agreements, save to the extent that the franchise agreements will imply requirements which are reflected in access agreements – for instance, for train paths.

Railtrack will have a network licence which will probably be issued by the Government in the first instance and will be administered by the Regulator.

Any party wishing to operate trains will require an operator licence. This applies to:

o British Rail residual passenger services;

o Franchised passenger service operators;

o Open access passenger service operators; and

o Freight train operators, all of whom will be open-access operators.

Some of the first of these may be issued by the Government but most will be issued by the Regulator and administered by him. It is through the operator's licence that the Regulator gains power over such matters as charges to passengers.

Any train operator will have to have an access agreement with Railtrack which, amongst many other things, will specify the charges to be paid to Railtrack. Every agreement must be approved by the Regulator. If a train operator fails to agree the terms of access with Railtrack, he can ask the Regulator to require Railtrack to enter into an agreement.

Station operators and train depot operators will also require operator licences. In addition, the Regulator will take an interest in codes of practice and standards, and in the contracts for the supply of goods and services by contractors to Railtrack and others.

He can vary licences by agreement: if not agreed he can refer the matter to the Monopolies and Mergers Commission.

The Regulator will ensure arrangements for allocating train paths and settling timetable disputes are fair and reasonable.

The Bill transfers to the Railway Regulator a number of the functions of the Director General of Fair Trading (DGFT) in respect of monopoly situations in the supply of Railway services. The Regulator can refer the supplier to the MMC.

He has rights to be consulted by Government, Franchising Director and others and rights to publish reports on the industry.

Amongst his principal duties are to:

o Promote economy and efficiency.

o Promote competition.

o Protect users and promote use of the network.

o Have regard to safety, the environment and the interests of the disabled.

o Not to render it unduly difficult for holders of network licences to finance their activities.

o Until December 1996 to take account of guidance from the Secretary of State.

o Impose minimum restrictions consistent with the performance of his functions.

o Enable providers of railway services to plan the future of their businesses with a reasonable degree of assurance.

As is normal in this kind of legislation, the Secretary of State (that is, in principle, *any* Secretary of State) retains the power to exempt operators and services from designations or requirements stipulated by either the Regulator or the Franchising Director. The main reason for this is to ensure the ability to exempt the bulk of London Underground services.

Policy Statements Additional to the Legislation

There have been two further important statements of policy.

Moderation of Competition

'The arrangements for gaining access should be structured to achieve the orderly and safe transfer to the private sector of British Rail's existing services at the earliest opportunity. The government recognises the potential tension between liberalising access for private sector operators and successfully franchising British Rail's existing passenger services. This means that to the extent necessary to ensure the success of the first generation of franchises, on-track competition between operators of passenger services may have to be moderated for a limited and specified period. The Government will at the outset of the new régime explain in respect of each group of services how and when it expects any initial moderation of competition to be removed.' (*Gaining Access...*, para.1.2.)

'[Competition] will be moderated, but only to the extent necessary to ensure the successful transfer of BR's passenger services to the private sector, and to ensure that the tax payer receives value for money for subsidising socially necessary services.' (*Gaining Access...*, para.6.5.)

Administered Pricing

Freight and open access passenger operators will negotiate access and prices with Railtrack on a commercial basis, subject to approval by the Regulator.

For franchised passenger operation, before each franchise operation the Franchising Director will arrange for the necessary train paths and agree their price with Railtrack. Any shortfall between that price and the successful operator's bid will be made up by subsidy. In the event that the bid exceeds the price the profit is to be paid into the Consolidated Fund.

Track access charges will have two components, a fixed and a variable component. The fixed component 'will cover those fixed costs which are directly attributable to the operator and an allocation of common costs'. The variable component will relate to 'the variable costs associated with frequency and timing' of services (*Gaining Access...*, para.6.9).

A bidder for a franchise will see:

o A service specification;

o The variable charge; and

o The rules on competition from other operators.

He will not be concerned with the fixed charge which will fall entirely to the Franchising Director – even though it may pass through his books it will not be material to him. The variable charge is only of interest insofar as the service specification allows him to vary, at his discretion, the service he offers.

Railtrack's income from the franchise is guaranteed by the Franchise Director who bears all the risks associated with the magnitude of the winning bid.

Therefore the basic decision-making consumer of infrastructure, who makes decisions about whether it is worthwhile paying the price asked for its use, is the Franchising Director, not the train operator.

Some of these features survive in the longer-term proposals. The differences are in the greater rôle taken by Railtrack in

'determining the way in which access rights are sold and will therefore bear more of the risks and rewards associated with its decision about how to package access rights for sale to operators'. (*Gaining Access...*, para.6.16).

This account indicates the importance for the economics of the outcome of the flexibility of the service specification, the split of charges between variable and fixed, the proportion of Railtrack's costs which are deemed to be common and the manner in which these common costs are recovered in the charges.

The Financial Régime

Setting up the financial régime for the new industry is complex. Some of the components are:

o The setting of the Franchising Director's budget.

o Railtrack's public expenditure totals: the three-year Investment and Financing Review and External Financing Limit. This in turn involves a view on Railtrack's internally generated income from charges, rentals, ancillary incomes and so forth. It also involves an investment plan.

o Income from charges will be heavily influenced by the rate of return required on Railtrack's inherited assets and on new investment.

o A view will have to be taken on the efficiency gains that can be expected from Railtrack and how these are to be secured. The mechanism for extracting these gains will have to be drafted into Railtrack's initial licence.

It is interesting to speculate what will 'give' in this financial structure when expectations on incomes and expenditures are not fulfilled, bearing in mind the relatively long-term nature of the legally binding contracts to be made by Railtrack and the Franchising Director for almost all of their outgoings, together with the year-to-year variation in funding for the industry which the Government has displayed in the past.

Construction of Access Charges for Franchised Operators

It is reasonably easy to agree a very general classification of infrastructure costs. There are costs which vary directly with the passage of a train such as traction power consumption and track damage. There are costs which are associated with the ability of a train to pass, such as long-term maintenance and replacement of track and signalling and the provision of capacity. These are referred to respectively as short-run and long-run avoidable costs. There are residual costs which cannot easily be attributed to any one activity for which I will use the term 'common costs'.

There is a considerable effort under way to identify what these elements of cost might be and then to translate them into a set of fair and efficient charges to train operators, which do not put Railtrack in the position of abuse of dominance in relation to operators, and do not distort unduly the terms of competition between train operators and other modes in final transport markets. The Regulator will approve these charges when he approves access agreements.

It is easy to say these things, but lifting the lid shows a fascinating set of problems for analysis. All I can do here is to pick out one or two rather broad issues which are amongst those which will have to be sorted out over the next few months.

Issues Outstanding

To what extent will traditional nationalised industry principles on accounting, depreciation and required rates of return be enforced?

The choice of the value of Railtrack's inherited assets and the rate of return to be earned on them together dictate a major part of Railtrack's income stream to be recovered from users. Assets are typically very long-lived and their current cost replacement values tend to exceed their historic cost valuations – implying high nominal rates of profit, even if real rates of profit are low. In the first instance these matters will be settled by the Government.

The application of Modern Equivalent Asset Value (MEAV) principles is attractive in principle for Railtrack's replaceable assets on the premise that there will be no closure. But there are some practical difficulties. For instance, what are correct asset lives to use? Is the approach appropriate for major stations which will be maintained rather than replaced? How does the long-term investment commitment implicit in the approach square with the variable three-year funding régime under which Railtrack will be operating as part of the public sector?

If it is recognised that closure is an option, then the assets in question will not be replaced and the question changes to short-term maintenance and alternative use value. If access charges are based on an MEAV basis, what happens if long-term aspirations are not fulfilled and assets are subsequently closed? Is there a regulatory interest in ensuring that Railtrack meaningfully relates its access charges to investment decisions?

A major issue is the mechanism for securing efficiency gains in Railtrack. It is for discussion whether an RPI-X type régime applied to access charges is appropriate, bearing in mind that there is no established set of prices to start with.

Like airports, Railtrack and its leaseholders will enjoy substantial income from property and trading. There are issues about the regulatory régime, if any, for these activities and about the extent to which these incomes are used to offset track and station access charges.

Railtrack will have responsibility for defining train paths and administering timetables. This is an immensely complex matter which provides opportunities for inadvertent and deliberate anti-competitive actions. The Regulator will need to have some way of satisfying himself that the processes used protect against such actions.

In the new, de-integrated structure, where will liability fall for losses and compensation to be paid due to equipment failure?

What should be the Franchising Director's criteria for choosing which services to subsidise and by how much within his given budget?

How will arrangements for through ticketing, and inter-availability of tickets between operators, be made?

There are several other issues such as the treatment of the peak, congestion and charges for any exclusive rights granted.[3]

Recovery of Common Costs

Much effort is being put into attributing costs to their causes. It remains to be seen what proportion of costs can be attributed, but I think that many of us would be surprised and pleased if it turned out to be more than 60 per cent *on average*. Since Railtrack has to break even and its main source of income is to be charges, it follows that 40 per cent or more of costs will have to be recovered in charges despite the fact that they are not related to any specific activity.

I have, of course, just been referring to an average figure. There will be isolated lines of route serving only one function whose total infrastructure costs would be avoidable by discontinuing the service. At the other extreme there will be services with shared facilities, a large proportion of whose costs are common.

This variation about the average raises a question about how geographically specific the reckoning of cost-recovery charges should be. One extreme option would be to derive one national total of costs, subtract a national total of attributed costs and then recover the difference from each charging unit.

This would have all sorts of implications, especially if the 'allocation' of the costs were to be done on a mechanical basis

---

[3] Some of these are discussed in my IEA paper with Tony Travers (1993).

connected with volume or size. Then services which already pay all their costs because they can be identified as avoidable would attract an additional proportion of the common costs incurred on behalf of services which had nothing to do with them. They would have an incentive to reduce their volume or size because that would avoid these charges. In some systems of allocation, free-standing freight lines would be contributing to passenger services, and rural passenger services would be contributing to complex urban networks. Ramsey-type principles of cost recovery might or might not support such an outcome.

The other extreme would be to ring-fence the common costs as tightly as possible to the geographical area in which they occur. Having done this one at least has options open on how best to recover the total.

Whilst it would not be realistic to attempt to apply Ramsey pricing and taxing principles in a rigorous and mechanistic manner, the general idea is fundamental to an outcome consistent with the notion of promoting the greatest overall use of the Railway. If one wishes to fund a lump-sum, in this case a lump of common costs, then one does least damage to economic efficiency by recovering more of it from the economically healthy parts of the system (ie those best able to sustain the charge as reflected in a relatively low elasticity of demand for rail services). John Collings and I (1978) showed many years ago that maximising the use of a public transport system in the simple sense of maximising the number of passenger miles, whilst meeting a lump-sum financial burden, produced Ramsey-like rules. We also observed in passing that our solution was essentially the same as the 'Social Fare' then being proposed for the Railways by Sir Peter Parker as a meaningful way of distributing government subsidy.

There will plainly be a limit on the degree to which unattributable costs can be disaggregated – otherwise there would be no problem. It is inevitable that some unattributable costs will have to be recovered. One might argue that in the case of franchised passenger services under administered pricing, the method used does not matter since the Franchising Director will end up paying the full amount in any case. However, it is desirable to attempt to establish and refine with the benefit of experience, economically efficient procedures which will work well in the longer term. In any case there are the non-franchised services to be dealt with.

When *allocating* costs, accountants look for a suitable measure by which to achieve the allocation. An obvious one in this case, which can be easily observed, is train mileage. One must accept that the procedures available are constrained by the data available and by what is practical. But to my mind there would be two disadvantages in recovering costs in this way.

First, from the train operator's point of view it would make most of this component of his charges move in direct proportion to his output, when, by definition, the relevant costs are not related to output.

Second, the measure would make no concession to the demand characteristics of the service as Ramsey principles would require. One importance of this stems from the variation in average train loads and profitabilities. Train miles-based recovery would make lightly loaded services, perhaps in the evenings, and on Sundays, incur high charges *relative* to the revenues. It would encourage the operator to withdraw the below-average revenue services even though these services might be capable of covering their avoidable costs and making some contribution to common costs.

If a simple rule is essential, then a passenger-mile or, better, passenger-revenue-based measure might be worth investigating.

Open-Access Charges

Finally, there is the question of the charges to be levied on open-access passenger and freight operators. The need for the freight charges is plain enough, but the need for open-access passenger charges should not be underestimated. Even if there are very few 'pure' open-access passenger train operators, it seems likely that there will be potential for established franchise holders to use spare resources to run open-access services over other franchise holders' patches. Of course, the extent to which this is permitted depends upon the extent of the Moderation of Competition enforced in the franchise agreements.

The proposition stated in *Gaining Access...* is that

> '[a]ll commercial operators ... will be expected to pay at least those "avoidable" costs that Railtrack would not incur if their service did not run. ... [I]f the remaining "common" costs were simply allocated on an averaged basis, more price-sensitive commercial traffic able only to meet avoidable costs would be priced off the railway. The result would be a declining traffic and higher charges. Therefore commercial freight operators will pay a negotiated charge, reflecting the value to them of using rail infrastructure. It will be subject to the oversight of the Regulator.' (*Gaining Access...*, para.4.1- 4.2)

The key concept here is that of a negotiated charge.

Passenger Fares

The Regulator may control fares through the operator licence. The duty, amongst others, to protect the interests of users of railway services will guide his exercise of these powers. Until the end of 1996, the Regulator has to take account of guidance from the Secretary of State.

Consultative Committees, which report to the Regulator, can comment on fares. The Regulator would be able to discharge his duties on fares either by making references to the Monopolies and Mergers Commission under his competition function or, more conveniently, by including a condition on fares in operators' licences.

The Franchising Director may control the fares of franchised operators through franchise agreements, and under a Commons amendment to the Bill he now has a duty to ensure, where the interests of users require it, that those fares are reasonable. The Franchising Director will be subject to guidance from the Secretary of State and directly accountable to him, and his annual budget will be determined through the normal process of negotiation with the Treasury. Expectations about fares levels will be reflected in the bids made by franchisees.

Therefore, fares on franchised passenger services are subject to two separate, independent forms of control. It remains to be seen how these control mechanisms work. To take but one example, an interesting situation might arise if the Franchising Director wished to raise fares on franchises in the London area in order to reduce the demands of the railway on the public purse, whilst the Regulator was unwilling to sanction the increase because of his duties to protect the consumer, to protect the environment and to promote the use of the railway.[4]

Competition Issues

The promotion of competition is one of the major objectives of the Regulator. It is the mechanism for delivering the benefits looked for from the policy.

Some would argue, however, that there is already too much competition rather than too little in both freight and local passenger transport markets. The old arguments talk of 'wasteful competition'

---

[4] Postscript: *The Guidance for the Rail Regulator, Objectives, Instructions and Guidance for the Franchising Director* and the *General Authority to the Rail Regulator* were issued at commencement on 1 April 1994. These make it clear that the primary responsibility for regulation of passenger fares for franchised services lies with the Franchising Director. He is to consult the Regulator.

and the unnecessary creation of excess capacity. The claim is that there is a 'need' for co-ordination. Personally, I have never been very impressed by these arguments. In the case of freight I suspect that the fiercely competitive market that has developed in road haulage has served its customers well, though it certainly has made life uncomfortable for the railways. Privatisation will refine ideas about the costs of taking various traffics – passenger and freight – and will show what has to be done in terms of improved efficiency if rail is to succeed in increasing its freight market share in markets where this is still a realistic prospect. It will also reveal the cost to the Exchequer, if any, of the Secretary of State's 'track charge grant scheme to assist freight traffic which cannot sustain even avoidable cost-based charges, and which would otherwise travel by road' (*Gaining Access...*, para.4.6).

It is for debate whether there is a case for recognising that there are some benefits from local agreements and monopolies in transport, which would normally fall foul of competition and fair trading law. I believe that the Office of Fair Trading is currently reviewing this topic in the context of the local bus industry.

The Regulator will have to formulate views on the terms which emerge from the negotiations for open-access freight and passenger services. The experience in the other regulators' offices will be particularly valuable here, especially in Telecoms. Whilst it might be nice to see the playing field tilted a little to encourage the entry of new operators – perhaps by relieving them of some of the 'normal' contribution towards unattributed costs – one must remember the prospect that much open-access passenger operation may come from franchised train operators working over each other's territory.

The policy of moderation of competition will have to be made operational. This will involve a fine judgement on the rights of exclusivity to be granted. Arguably it would be better to err on the side of granting more monopoly rights than strictly necessary in the interests of making sure something happens. Much of the value of monopoly rights may be recovered in the prices bid for them. But, of course, this runs counter to the desire for competition.

It should not be forgotten that a major part of the new policy is to introduce competition into procurement and all other aspects of the *Railtrack* business. This could be an important source of efficiency gain – perhaps the most important source. It will entail a myriad of contracts, with one of the parties a state-owned monopsony operating under regulation. It remains to be seen what issues this creates for the Regulator.

The analogy with competitive procurement in the public sector and, in particular, competitive tendering of London buses provides useful information on the effects that supply-side competition can have.

Rail Freight Rate Regulation in the United States

The regulation of rail freight access charges is a particularly difficult and interesting matter. The US system may have some useful ideas.

The US system has several features which are designed to encourage parties to reach agreements amongst themselves and to limit severely the number of cases which come up for formal determination.

o Subject to the protection of captive customers, the legitimacy of – and need for – non-abusive price discrimination by rail companies, reflecting supply and demand, is explicitly recognised;

o Where both parties agree, railways are empowered to enter into binding legal contracts with customers: *these contracts are immune from regulatory scrutiny*;

o Protection of captive shippers is achieved *by placing a requirement on carriers to issue posted tariffs* – subject to regulatory scrutiny – for most freight services. Carriers must offer the same terms to any shipper who falls under a particular tariff and the tariff rates may not be unreasonably high. Captive customers, therefore, have access to a regulated tariff as an alternative to an unregulated bilateral contract with carriers.

The rules and guidelines which limit the Interstate Commerce Commission's (ICC's) jurisdiction over tariff rates and guide its judgement over rate reasonableness are as follows:

o *First*, regulatory jurisdiction has to be established by determining whether the carrier's revenue-to-variable-cost ratio for the traffic in question exceeds 180 per cent. This test has proved to be an effective mechanism for reducing regulatory appeals.

o *Second*, if there is jurisdiction, the ICC has to determine whether the carrier is market dominant with respect to traffic which moves under the tariff in question, defined as 'the absence of effective competition from other carriers or modes of transportation'. There are four major relevant forms of competition:

o existence of an effective rail alternative;

o intermodal competition;

o geographical competition: an alternative destination or source;

o product competition: availability of a substitute product.

o *Third*, if there is market dominance, the ICC has to determine maximum rates. There are *ad hoc* guidelines for non-coal traffic and formalised guidelines for coal traffic, known as constrained market pricing.

Constrained Market Pricing

On 8 August 1985 the US Interstate Commerce Commission issued its Coal Rate Guideline, Nationwide. This had evolved over a period of years to become a sophisticated application of relevant economic principles to practical regulation of rate-making:

'The Commission adopts "Constrained Market Pricing" (CMP) to serve as guidelines for determining the reasonableness of rail captive coal rates. ... A captive coal shipper should not be required to pay more than is necessary for the rail carriers involved to earn adequate revenues. Nor should it pay more than is necessary for efficient service. A captive coal shipper should not bear the costs of any facilities or services from which it derives no benefit. Responsibility for payment for facilities or services which are shared (to its benefit) by other shippers should be apportioned according to the demand elasticities of the various shippers. Thus railroads would be given incentives to ensure that competitive traffic contributes as much as possible toward these costs. Finally, changes in coal rates should not be so precipitous as to cause severe economic dislocations.'

'Taken together, these constraints should ensure that a carrier does not use its market dominance to charge its captive coal shippers more than they should have to pay for efficient rail service. A shipper will not be asked to subsidize long-term excess capacity, fund revenue shortfalls which could be eliminated by pricing the costs associated with avoidable operating inefficiencies. Carriers will be effectively limited in the rates they can charge on captive traffic and will have the necessary incentive to maximise the net revenue contribution from competitive traffic. Cross-subsidization of other shippers is effectively precluded. We expect the rate structure resulting from the interaction of market forces and the constraints we have described to produce rates that are economically efficient and fair to all shippers.'

The ICC coal rate guidelines are soundly based on principles of economic efficiency. They embody the ideas behind Ramsey pricing, but in a flexible and non-mechanistic fashion. They have the appearance of being fair and reasonable.

Conclusion

The following features make the railway case special.

From the point of view of those interested in regulation as a subject, the most significant new feature is that an independent regulator is being set up to deal with an industry which will very largely stay in the public sector, at least in its formative stages. Railtrack will remain a nationalised industry, but also the Franchising Director, Railtrack's most important customer, has his budget determined by the Government. Anybody who has experienced the workings of a nationalised transport industry from the inside will immediately recognise the significance of this: it is inevitable, and quite right that there will be debates when £1,000 million every year of public money is at issue. For this reason alone we are in uncharted waters.

The industry is loss making and some sectors are declining: hence the franchising solution, which is new.

There is a wide range of profitability and considerable cross-subsidy within the railway system in order to preserve unremunerative service beyond what external financial support would sustain. Commercial costing and competition will expose this. No major technical innovation is in prospect (unlike Telecoms) which would fundamentally alter opportunities for competition within the railways. Similarly, there is not much in prospect for fundamental technological innovation in the transport industry as a whole. It is a labour-intensive industry and still a large employer – so costs are heavily affected by general real earnings in the long term. Prices of material inputs are of less significance than in gas or electricity.

The product is heterogeneous: many quite different products are sold under the general description of railway service. Delivered product quality is fundamentally more variable and difficult to measure and monitor: but it matters to consumers. The different situations pose different regulatory problems. The BR Sectors summarise some of the differentiating characteristics, but there is enormous within-sector variation. Usage is very unevenly spread in the population – though many people have particularly strong feelings about railways.

There are no established prices for things like the use of railway infrastructure. These must be established in the absence of any kind of market before a price capping formula can be contemplated. Similarly, there will be no flotation of the infrastructure assets which could give information about their valuation for the purpose of discussing rates of return.

Charging is complex. There are a great number of non-standard transactions which impose significant costs on passengers and suppliers. This is one of the reasons for the sensitivity of the through-ticketing issue.

In many segments of the relevant markets for travel and goods transport, competition is already intense and the railway is almost entirely deregulated. There is a real risk of ending up with more economic regulation rather than less in these cases. In some segments there is genuine market power in the railway and there is already considerable regulation of user charges and service quality, some of it powerful but informal.

Conflicts and Ambiguities

A number of inherent conflicts and ambiguities will have been noted in what I have described. They are recognised by Government and I think they are a natural symptom of new policies under development in a technically and politically complex situation.

There is a valiant attempt to set up charging, accounting, regulatory systems which will give sensible economic signals about which activities are worth expanding and which should be contracted. Meanwhile, 'administered pricing', 'moderation of competition' are being developed as policies which, in the short run at least, are designed to defeat market signals by rendering them irrelevant.

Arguably, a major benefit of the railways policy will be to expose the present pattern of subsidies to public scrutiny, through the decisions taken by the Franchising Director in the light of his budget, the access charges he faces and the value of bids received for franchises. It is my personal view that it is entirely right that the magnitude of the subsides to particular activities should be exposed for debate, and that as a result many people will question whether there are better ways of spending the same public money within the railway, or public transport, system.

There is a tension between the general desire on the part of government to reduce public expenditure on railways like everything else, and the recognition that the efficiency benefits of rail privatisation will take time to realise. In the meantime, public expenditure cuts would be unfairly blamed on the privatisation policy and would also make it harder to execute successfully.

The promotion of competition has been accepted as the over-riding objective of other regulators, and this is also the case with railways. But even where moderation of competition may not be strictly necessary to ensure the sale of franchises, competition will imply loss of current local monopoly profits, which would increase the demands on the public purse if they were to be replaced by direct state support. This creates a tension between the desire for competition for the benefit of the consumer and the desire to restrict it for the benefit of the tax-payer. This is familiar from the other privatisations.

Responsibilities to control fares are being created in a complex way. There is a risk that failure to recognise that many rail markets are already highly competitive will lead to attempts to control prices to final consumers (fares and freight charges) in a way which would upset competition, not help it. The proposals as they now stand are inherently flexible. Franchising can proceed quickly or slowly depending on the response of the market and on how policy – and funding – develops. The railway is a large and diverse set of services and different structures must be created to suit the differing circumstances.

More complete privatisation would make the new industry more immune from interference but it is inevitable that the existence of subsidy will slow change down. It is to be hoped the Government is able to resist pressures to intervene in the market or quasi-market mechanisms that are to be created. This would be to risk undermining the achievements and improvements which privatisation could bring.

BIBLIOGRAPHY

Department of Transport (1992): White Paper, *New Opportunities for the Railways*, Cm.2012, London: HMSO, July.

Department of Transport (1993): *Gaining Access to the Railway Network,* DoT Consultation Document, February.

Glaister, S., and J.J. Collings (1978): 'Maximisation of Passenger-Miles in Theory and Practice', *Journal of Transport Economics and Policy*, September.

Glaister, S., and T. Travers (1993): *New Directions for British Railways? The Political Economy of Privatisation and Regulation,* IEA Current Controversies No.5, London: Institute of Economic Affairs.

CHAIRMAN'S COMMENTS

Sir Christopher Foster
Coopers and Lybrand

I SPEAK AS ONE HEAVILY INVOLVED in rail privatisation, spending about a third of my time on it as special advisor to the Secretary of State. My task tonight is as a brief discussant so that everybody can open up.

First, is rail privatisation different? Yes, it certainly is. All privatisations are different, all cases of regulations are different, but they have family resemblances.

One difference is that about a hundred different businesses are being created, most of them for sale. And one set of issues, which we may come back to, is the structure; Stephen did not, I think, mention vertical integration. In my judgement, the argument against vertical integration, which has dominated discussions, is a belief in the distinction between a command economy and a contractual one. The balance of advantage in this case is in replacing command relationships with contractual ones. That is the prime reason why there is a separation between Rail Track and the franchises. But there are a number of questions about structure which are being worked on.

Next, is there as much competition as possible? You have stressed that in a sense every franchise is going to be able to procure its rolling stock competitively, and many engineering services. Rail Track is also going to be able to procure its engineering and maintenance services competitively. There are lots of smaller businesses, now supplied on a 'you have got to have me' kind of basis within BR, that are in future going to be supplied competitively.

The proposed franchising, that is, competition for the ground, so to speak, rather than on the ground, is a difference from earlier privatisations. Here, a major issue is to what extent there shall be a competitive free-for-all from the start. My understanding is that Ministers are anxious to have as much competition as possible, but that, on the other hand, there is a question of how much uncertainty over the extent of competition is consistent with what the City will find saleable. That particular tension is going to have to be worked out over the next few months.

Why not sell the assets rather than franchise them? Stephen has given one reason, which is subsidy. But there is also the important point that nobody believes that the exact pattern of services is at the optimum, nor that very much about British Rail is optimal. In crude terms, that is the reason for what you are reluctant to call 'privatisation'. So, given that the Government has committed itself to continuing with the present level of subsidies, insofar as that is necessary to maintain the present level of services, the issue is, can one find better ways of delivering these services which also require less subsidy, or patterns of services, more in the passenger's interest, which imply less subsidy?

But another reason for franchising rather than sale, which I think you did not mention, is that the really long-term investment is by Rail Track. It is not practical to invest very long term in either rolling stock or Rail Track through a short-run vehicle; on the other hand, if one wants to get competition in and bring about private sector ways of doing things, one needs a short-term vehicle.

An important issue, I think, is the motivation of Rail Track. Why on earth would you expect the public sector body to have any incentive to get rid of any of these costs, or make cost savings? To which I think the answer is that, even though it is going to be a public sector body, it will be highly incentivised in a way that public sector bodies have not been in the past. Moreover, it will shortly be privatised. Above all, we should talk about where the cost savings are to come from, because, in the end, getting rid of productive inefficiency in the system is going to be the main source of customer benefits.

8

ABUSE OF MONOPOLY POWER

Professor M E Beesley
London Business School

Introduction

I DEAL IN THIS LECTURE with one aspect of pro-competition legislation – countering abuse of monopoly power held by a single, or few, interests. This choice is in part because the other main area of the legislation – countering collective monopoly power – has been a central concern of UK legislation since the original Monopolies and Restrictive Practices Commission (now MMC) focused on it in the early 1950s. That area is rather easily aligned with European Commission procedures, a motive which has strongly influenced discussions on current reform. But it is mostly because, after all the brave words of the November 1992 Green Paper on *Abuse of Monopoly Power*, which I will call *AMP* for short, there is a good question of whether a mouse has appeared – namely, the new measures announced by Mr Hamilton in April this year.

I review the options in the November paper, to compare the possibilities mooted there with what was actually selected. Then I canvass possible reasons for the omissions, stressing in particular the failure of the review process to deal adequately both with principles and the evidence on practices available to it. From this, I suggest a revised agenda for reform. I hope this will stimulate a useful debate in an area in which none of us can claim to be all-wise.

What Is the Problem to Be Tackled?

Before embarking on the comparison, an excursion into some relevant concepts will be helpful. What *is* the problem with which we want regulation to help? By 'regulation' I mean at this point any means intended to bear on commercial decisions in specific markets, whether they be administrative or legal. Whether one means is more apt than another should emerge from analysis of the task deemed to be necessary. In practice, the potential task is to intervene in relations between an incumbent or incumbents and entrants and would-be entrants, entrants who will wish to expand. For convenience, I shall henceforth speak in the singular, to epitomise what is usually thought of as market power.

The task is likely to arise in the following way. In general, I believe we may rely on Schumpeter's perennial gale of creative destruction to undermine monopoly.[1] Indeed, we have no choice; the vast bulk of capitalist rivalry happens in that way – and certainly before governmental processes can perceive problems which need to be addressed. The task arises where there is an established and successful incumbent, whose market position may be attacked. The possibility of anti-social behaviour by the incumbent is strongly related to the conditions of symmetry or asymmetry as between incumbent and entrant, and how these bear on each party's search for profit.

Symmetry, or lack of it, applies to each of the principal dimensions determining profit – revenues and outlays. In general, entry becomes more problematical (and of dubious worth) the greater the symmetry between incumbent and entrant on each of the profit determinants. At the limit, we have identical demand-cost conditions as seen by each. This is the set-up beloved of modern industrial economics, in which the entry problem can be reduced to a kind of timeless game between incumbent and entrant. To be sure, some deviation from symmetry can be, and is, explored, and with great elaboration. But its starting point – symmetry – makes the analyses of small actual assistance in our problem. The real world is likely to display a great variation in the conditions, and takes place in real time. The incumbent, by definition, is already *there*. The problem is not at the extremes of the spectrum of symmetry to asymmetry. Profit makers are deterred if they perceive neither a cost nor a market advantage relative to the incumbents; they will not trouble a regulator; they will not think it worth while to take the risk. At the other extreme, regulation is irrelevant; incumbents will be relatively powerless to affect the search for profit. So regulation has to inhabit the half-world of partial overlap on the profit dimensions as between incumbents and entrants. This, as we shall see, has important consequences for the possible reform of regulation.

---

[1] J.A. Schumpeter, *Capitalism, Socialism and Democracy*, New York: Harper & Row, 1942.

The Green Paper's Concerns

The Green Paper[2] was concerned with conduct aimed at potential or existing entrants, and the consequences of incumbent power deemed unattackable, and therefore requiring price and/or quality control. There was some unnecessary confusion between these requirements by referring to the first as 'anti-competitive' and the second as 'exploitative' conduct. The principal dimensions of an 'effective' system were described as 'adequate powers to investigate and remedy abuse' aimed at stifling competition 'in different market structures and in all areas of economic activity'. It should deter abuse as well as tackling detected abuses. The system should be clear and certain in its application and should not unduly burden business or inhibit entrepreneurial behaviour. 'There may be benefits in aligning this aspect of competition law with EC law and the laws of other member-states.'

Respondents to the Green Paper were offered a choice between three options, the tests of which were proposed as:

o effective deterrence and control;

o range of conduct embraced; and

o complexity and therefore cost to companies (and to governments!).

The three options comprised:

(i)   strengthening the existing system;

(ii) a prohibition system; and

(iii) a dual system.

Deterrence was deemed a function of:

o scope for private action;

o investigative power;

o power to impose fines for abuse; and

---

[2] *Abuse of Monopoly Power*, Department of Trade and Industry, London: HMSO, November 1992.

o the ability to order divestment remedies, or, alternatively, price control.

Range or scope was a function of the ability to tackle respectively:

o exploitative behaviour;

o anti-competitive behaviour;

o joint dominance (that is, parallel action between incumbents);

o market power based on property rights; and

o the market share level at which actions could be triggered.

The likely cost was judged in terms of conformity with EC or existing UK powers, and thus the weight of regulation burden on firms; and the costs of administration to be shouldered by the government.

There is some overlap between these dimensions which need not detain us; but a comment on the concern about the property rights is perhaps needed. At first sight, restraint on the use of these rights could be construed as a remarkably radical suggestion, considering the prominent rôle of property rights in explaining market power. It appears, however, that what was in mind was rather limited transactions based on land (the example given, which is already in the scope of UK laws, was grants of rights in land to be used in letting pitches for holiday caravans). The potential Pandora's box opened up by thus addressing a basic problem of monopoly power was not explored in the Green Paper. That is a symptom of one of the main limitations of the whole exercise, namely, failure to consider how underlying barriers to entry could or should be tackled, which I shall consider, alongside other limitations, later. (I do not intend to open the box, either, in this lecture – at least not directly.)

Annex C of the Green Paper evaluated the three options, and do-nothing (the current system) on a four-point scale from weakest to strongest. I reproduce it here.

Annex C

Option 1 meant:

o giving OFT stronger investigative powers;

o greater coverage of property rights;

o scope for the DGFT to accept binding undertakings in order to shorten investigation;

o provision for damages, and 'perhaps' civil penalties (but *not* private actions, as Annex C makes clear; these were to be reserved for Options 2 and 3).

The proposal was to link undertakings with the point at which the Director General of Fair Trading (DGFT) refers a case of abuse to the Monopolies Commission (under the 1980 Act), that is, where the firm whose conduct is complained of has failed to concede to DGFT's proposed remedies.

Option 2 envisaged a wholesale substitution of the 1973 and 1980 Act procedures to mirror as closely as possible the Article 86 provisions of the Treaty of Rome. Prominent among them are prohibitions of specific conduct backed up by fines and appeal to the European Court. But Article 86's scope would be widened in the UK case to catch parallel action among a few incumbents ('joint dominance', now limited in European law to cases of common ownership or specific agreements). The Green Paper clearly wished at this point to side-step the present difficulties of dealing with 'complex monopolies' under the 1973 Act, by referring to a 'narrower focus than the sectoral investigations under-taken in the monopoly provisions' (p.9). Remedies would include divestment and price controls. It might be possible to have a trigger at a lower level than that (40 per cent market share) deemed 'dominant' under Article 86. Fines along 86 lines could be imposed (up to 10 per cent of turnover).

Option 3, the dual system, essentially added to Option 2, specifically to preserve, alongside the Article 86 derivatives, the present powers of MMC for 'in depth investigation', including investigation of close oligopoly. This would also bring in divestiture and price control as remedies.

After the Green Paper

I will not go into the views expressed in the consultation, except to remark that collectively they are a striking testimony to the insights of the public choice theorists. Each interest – including regulators, general or specific, not only commercial and industrial interests – argued for the system most suited to its individual position. Its lines of criticism and its constructive suggestions followed. A wide range of opinion duly emerged, leaving the government more or less where it had been before the whole exercise, but giving plenty of scope to justify particular outcomes in terms of representations. In the event, Mr Hamilton announced, in effect, that the choice was Option 1 – with some modi-fication. He 'would build on the strengths of the existing legislation' instead of more radical action.

I wish to comment at this point on the three most important proposed changes, namely: first, stronger investigative powers, to enable the DGFT to establish more quickly whether there should be a full invest-igation; what these are has yet to be disclosed. Two specifically involve the Competition Act. The DG is to be enabled to accept enforceable undertakings before his formal investigation under the Competition Act, and in lieu of a monopoly reference under the Fair Trading Act. Breach would be enforceable in the Courts. This presumably is also to be a trigger for civil actions for damages. Also he is to be able to make interim orders under the Competition Act which would prohibit specified activities where a complainant 'risked suffering serious damage during the period of the MMC investigation'.

Thus the present two-stage procedure of investigation – the DGFT's and the MMC's, after a reference – was to be preserved, with the differences that the DGFT would have a stronger hand to seek compli-ance, both directly on seeking enforceable orders before his 'full scale investigation' and later, with respect to referring disputed findings to the MMC. Reaching the latter stage was to be made more formidable to incumbents because of the possible effect of interim orders during the MMC's investigation. The obvious implication is an intention to increase the DGFT's powers, in that, because the prospective penalties are to be higher, the probability of an incumbent accepting under-takings are also increased. One effect of this, as I am sure was part of the intention, is to lessen both DGFT's and MMC's burden of work. It was not made clear whether, as now, the DGFT's investigation would be published, but it seems to be likely that it would not. I understand that the DGFT's powers are to be borrowed at least in part from his merger powers, which do not provide for publication of his findings. Perhaps more significant an addition to his Competition Act armoury is the power to negotiate specific changes in behaviour by the incumbent in lieu of a reference to the MMC.

What was not spelled out was the nature of the undertakings the DGFT was to be able to require. His powers in mergers stem princip-ally from the ability to negotiate a modification of a proposed merger, in particular by persuading the parties to divest that part of their joint activities liable substantially to increase market power. This ability to negotiate divestment does not sound like a mouse. But, as applied to suspected AMP, it is surely too much of a steam-hammer to be wielded without a full MMC investigation. One of the conveniences of these proposals is that, as again I understand it, they can be incorporated in the forthcoming deregulation bill. This is convenient, especially in view of the fact that, thanks to pressure on Parliamentary slots, one could not reasonably expect new legislation to deal with the whole pro-competitive area at least for the next (1994-95) session of Parliament.

So now we have collected at least three items calculated to provoke discussion: If indeed there is to be a significant increase in the DGFT's influence, is there to be a commensurate increase in accountability to balance it? Maybe this, however, will also be dealt with under the bill. (Perhaps someone will tell us!) Second, we have what some would regard as the paradoxical position that legislation on Restrictive Trade Practices is to be delayed, while some reform of dealing with abuse is given priority. Perhaps Sir Gordon Borrie was aware of this in his recent urgent plea to get moving on the former. But I wish at this point to concentrate on a third question – has enough been proposed for dealing with AMP?

The Green Paper's Verdict

As we saw, the announcement sticks closely to Option 1, so the Green Paper verdict on the Government's response to its concerns has already been given, in effect, in Annex C. As we can see, on deterrence and scope of power, Option 3 dominated Option 2 in the ranking. Option 1 is deemed 'fairly weak' on deterrence, 3 is strongest. The scope of 2 and 3 is identical. Option 1 is clear in its expected operation; Option 3 is 'uncertain initially' here. So the Green Paper's *ex ante* verdict must have been that the choice for Option 1 trades off better deterrence in favour of saving costs of operation, including that of reducing regu-latory uncertainty, which would be relevant mainly in the short run. Specifically, more complicated overlaps between UK and EC powers and increase in the 'regulatory burden' on firms would be avoided.

There was to be, it seems, no new help to private actions beyond that which could follow breach of undertakings, and no fines which would follow prohibition of nominated, but 'illustrative' items of conduct, such as those emerging under EC case law, as in the Green Paper's Options 2 and 3. These are the familiar themes of objectionable con-duct which, by now, include discriminatory pricing, fidelity rebates, oppressive discount policies, predatory pricing, tie-in pricing, and with-holding supplies, as found in particular commercial situations. The ground for rejection of prohibition was given as the difficulty of assessing in advance what will be regarded as anti-competitive, and what is acceptable, behaviour. Also 'a prohibition would bite on fewer market situations than our present legislation'. The latter point was unfair to Green Paper Option 3, which would not, like 2, leave everything to an EC look-alike.

Thus, the obvious question about what is intended which is raised by the Green Paper's analysis is the rejection of its emphasis on deter-rence. But the prior question must be: What was conspicuously missing from the Green Paper's analysis in the first place, and what, if any, lessons should have emerged? My own problems with the Green Paper were its failure to start with the fundamentals of large firm power, and its failure to ask what were the weaknesses of the Competition Act in particular, weaknesses which are only very partially addressed by the DGFT's proposed new powers. It also failed to take on board the question of altering company behaviour in the area I have defined as critical, namely, what to do (if anything) when there is considerable, but not too much, asymmetry of conditions facing the incumbent and entrant. The characteristic beliefs of incumbents in these situations will be that, on the demand side, there are no worthwhile unexpected 'y' inefficiencies they have neglected, that is, entry to the market must be rivalrous, and seriously damage profit prospects, and on the cost side, a firm disbelief in the possibility of 'x' inefficiency. Entrants will tend to believe the opposite. The competitive public interest question is: Will intervention to increase the probability of entry be beneficial, net, to consumers?

Complementing the Green Paper's Analysis

Most of us assent to the view that the essence of incumbent power is entry barriers, ranging over a vast array of possibilities, from unique property rights, and government regulation, to those immediately affecting the incumbents' costs, and in particular sunk costs which entrants may have to face, but incumbents do not. A 'barrier to entry' denotes a particular condition of asymmetry between incumbents and entrants favourable to the former. Correspondingly, an aim of creating more competition should address the question of whether, and how, the barriers can be lowered – while of course at the same time taking on board the reality that the new competitors, too, will require their own means of defending, for a suitable time, the quasi-rents which induce them to enter. Obviously, one way to encourage entry (depending on the entrant's own needs for defence) is to lower the barriers. The scope for general competition authorities to do this unilaterally is often quite narrow – so much depends on other legislation, other sponsoring Departments, and so on, and will often require primary legislation. In practice, the need is for regular review of legislative and other entry barriers as revealed in monopoly cases, so that suitable pressures to reform can be mounted. (The scope is rather wider for utility regulators, who can do more to negotiate to alter the rules set out in licences or authorisations; but they too in the end will hit the buffer of the requirement for primary legislation if they wish to do more than using the licence mechanism allows.)

The scope for conduct amounting itself to a barrier for newcomers depends on the underlying asymmetry of rights. The potential use of conduct by an incumbent to create a barrier is by acquiring a reputation for behaviour which will sacrifice his profit. If this is not backed by underlying barriers of other kinds, this reputation will not survive long as a barrier itself.[3] The more important possibility is making use of that part of the entry conditions which are common, in order to deter those which are not. It is clear then that, in the real world, judgements about what is, and what is not, likely to affect entry by prohibition of aspects of conduct is a very nice one, calling for a good deal of expertise and commercial knowledge in working out what will be its effects.

So far as this argument goes, then, the government was right to reject the idea of nominating forbidden items of conduct for prohibition in advance. It throws equal doubt, however, on the practicality and efficacy of any 'interim orders'. The snag is the proviso that there must be 'good reason to believe' in damage to an entrant. This is rarely, if ever, possible before a thorough investigation, which must be very exacting. If ever there are to be items of conduct 'prohibitable' *ex ante*, these, I would argue, must emerge from a series of test cases, as they do, in effect, from EC case law. There are, of course, also the familiar arguments for such tests more appropriately to emerge from a formal legal process rather than as part of administrative process. Since I doubt whether conduct can be usefully codified in that way, I think the use of the courts is more important in other aspects of the problem, as we shall see.

---

[3] There is an analogy here with restrictive trade practices. Entry can be deterred by an agreement to deter but this agreement will not last long without props based on underlying entry barriers.

Weaknesses of Competition Act 1980 – Green Paper's Failure

The second failure of the Green Paper was to consider systematically where the Competition Act 1980 was weak. In particular, it failed to draw the lessons available from the utility regulators' origins, structure and experience. They were regarded, it seems, as interests to be negotiated with rather than to be learned from. The powers given to the specialist regulators (Oftel, Ofgas, Offer, etc.) in important measure stemmed from the perceived weaknesses in the Competition Act. In each case, the judgement was made that the Act was inadequate to deal with an incumbent starting off its privatised existence with 100 per cent market share. The objective possibilities of competition, and its speed of development, varied widely among the several regulators' industries. One might, for example, have expected the Green Paper to have given special attention to Telecoms, where potential for competition was strongest, and the track record of dealing with an incumbent longest.

Telecom is a good witness to my thesis of the importance of asymmetry in entry problems. For example, though it has been possible to mimic existing voice services since simple resale was allowed in 1989, there is very little interest in doing so – there is little profit in it. On the other hand cellular, substantially innovative, grew rapidly. Cable operators can add their telecom business to an independent market, cable TV. Personal Communication Network (PCN) offers are in the gap between Cellular and POTS ('plain old telephone service'). But all, of course, also depend on incumbent services, prices, etc., to operate. Here lies the main regulatory work. The big initial entrant, Mercury, which *was* meant as an intended duplicate of the incumbent, was in effect trying to substitute for what *should* have been done before privatisation, namely, vertical, and to some degree horizontal, divestment of the incumbent. A corollary of negotiating an entry of that degree of parallelism with the incumbent, was that a doctrine of subsidy for entry through favourable interconnect terms had to be put in place, even if covertly. The idea of 'help' for entrants in this way is very dubious. It is far better to rely on anti-trust principles to encourage competitors. And we have to live with the difficult consequences of such a deal when further entrants come along, as Martin Cave's paper showed.

I think telecoms, and indeed all the other specialist regulators' experience, would also have pointed to another asymmetry – that of information between the Regulator and incumbent, and to a lesser extent that between incumbent and entrant about demand and cost conditions in the industry. There is no question in this respect where the advantage initially lies. It is with the incumbent. On the other hand, the Regulator starts off with a clear but virtually uninformed mind; the would-be entrant does not know, at the beginning, much in detail about whether opportunities along the demand or cost dimensions will be worth the risk of commitment. I come back to the problem of how learning could be made speedier later. Here, I wish to note that more by happy accident than design, the regimes have turned out to be rather good – some would say too much so – in dealing effectively with the incumbent/entrant interface.

Partly this is due to the licence or authorisation which the Regulators police.The licence terms announce general categories of potentially abusive behaviour (undue discrimination, tie-in behaviour, undue preference for one's own ownership interest, and so on) but wisely refrain from being specific. Regulatory action is triggered by entrants' complaints. A recent Telecoms example is reported in *Oftel News* (24 September 1993), giving an insight into what is implied in running such a system. The incumbent in this case was Mercury, defending its Mercury One-2-One service, which had its own licence. Complaints concerned: offering terms putting newcomers wishing to resell Mercury One-2-One capacity at a disadvantage to Mercury's own direct sales division, unfair advantages in provision of handsets, and unfair cross-subsidy of handsets. Don Cruickshank decided, initially, that these were unfounded fears. But the striking thing for my argument is that all this took place *before* Mercury launched Mercury One-2-One; and that though, *prima facie*, there was no intended excessive undue preference, more information for Mercury One-2-One bearing on the entrant DSB's profitability could be and was exacted, so that the regulator could consider the case further.

The moral is: effective real-time intervention on behalf of entrants requires a continuously acting regulator able to decide promptly on the implications for both incumbents' and entrants' profits. But I find it inconceivable – whatever its merits in the telecoms case, and these are undoubted – that this type of action and its context (a licence attuned to the general needs of the entrants) would be replicated to deal with all possible cases of 'abuse' in the commercial world at large. The costs would be prohibitive. One should try to incorporate the specialist regulators' ability to influence company decisions, as far as possible, in the general law.

A Programme for Reform

So the lessons for AMP I would draw from the specialist regulators' experience are: *first*, that experiences would have indicated the necessary conditions for exacting 'undertakings', the main innovation proposed for adding to the 1980 Act. Undertakings certainly work in the regulators' cases, but only because of the framework in which they are set – namely, of licences, with the credible threat of reference to MMC, which will escalate the possible disadvantages of not agreeing. I do not think that it will be practicable for the DGFT to repeat the success he had when he was the Telecoms regulator with the newly proposed powers for his present office. The necessary framework is missing.

Second, the regulators' and the MMC's experience is very useful in indicating how relevant evidence in monopoly cases can be revealed. Much was made in the Green Paper and subsequent discussions of the need to strengthen powers of investigation on the EC model. I would make a distinction here between the evidence of a kind conclusive, or nearly so, in itself (the 'smoking gun') and that which needs to be interpreted, often subtly, in a context. The first type is more likely to be found by the 'dawn raid' if collusion among firms is a condition of exercising power – that is, in Restrictive Trade Practices cases. There, as widely agreed, the additional powers will be useful. The MMC (and the regulators) have wide powers to call up evidence, backed by sanctions they very rarely (if at all) have to invoke. Neither, it seems, feels that its present powers are inadequate. They consider, rightly, that the utility needs of interpreting conduct are adequately served by their ability to hear from all interested parties, and their ability to consider many hypotheses about conduct.

However, it is again true that the regulators are those who have to work day-by-day on the coal face of incumbent/entrant problems. It has turned out that in this work the burden of proof has been critical. The effect of general prohibitions in the licence conditions is, of course, to shift the burden of proof – to disprove a hypothesis about conduct – on to the incumbent. This mechanism notably increases information provision, thus substantially reducing the disadvantage from which regulators suffer when they commence operations. Again, I do not think the proposed stronger powers of investigation match up to this experience.

The important question here, of course, which always raises lively debate, is whether a shifting of the burden of proof to incumbents could or should be adopted for application in the general competition laws. I think there is no doubt that if it is to be done, it has to be in the framework of a court, or the nearest equivalent. Since I also think the chances of a substantial shift towards substituting the High Court for present administrative procedures approach zero, desirable as it might be in principle, we have to look to the MMC still to perform the function of weighing up the evidence. To what extent, however, can the MMC operate more effectively without the formal framework that is available to the specialist regulators to evoke evidence? Here I must be careful not to fulfil the expectations of the public choice theorists by special pleading! I must say, however, that what has impressed me most in my time at the MMC is the breadth and depth of experience the members bring to their task. I certainly view them as capable of sorting out the very tricky question of interpreting conduct in cases of entry asymmetry; indeed, they are probably uniquely capable. The MMC's strength here really depends much more on its collective business judgement than on the economic analyses it prompts, though both are necessary. This judgement would be very difficult to replicate in the High Court. Thus I envisage more monopoly references for the MMC in cases where the DGFT suspects abuse, not less.

But I think a change in the MMC's procedure here would do much to reinforce its ability to evoke the kind of evidence possible with the burden of proof upon the incumbent. I have in mind promoting, and putting earlier in an inquiry, the exploration of remedies, thus making them more integral to the MMC's learning process. It would then also be possible to narrow down remedies early enough to put them to the parties more firmly, inviting more and richer arguments in rebuttal where the incumbent (or incumbents) disagree. The Commission's final proposal – and its wider observations on matters affecting entry – would be the more effective.[4]

Asymmetry of Information

I pointed also to the asymmetry of information as between incumbent and entrant. In a practical case, reducing this is critical to an entrant's profit calculations. I do not refer here to a knowledge of the incumbent's intentions. In a competitive economy, each actor is entitled to keep his own counsel about strategy. The need for correcting the

---

[4] Traditionally, the MMC has proceeded by first making its inquiries, hearing evidence from the referred 'monopolist' and any other interested parties, deciding on the basic question of whether the conduct that is revealed is against the public interest, and if so then proposing 'remedies' on which the 'monopolist' makes observations rather late in the inquiry.

imbalance is simply overcoming the problem that the incumbent *is* largely the industry, holding extremely valuable data in assessing its potential. There is a need to tackle this obstacle which goes to the wider problem of disclosure of commercial information.

In the UK, as in the EC, far too much weight is put on so-called protection of commercially sensitive material. And it is no better than it used to be. It may well be true, for example, that the numbers of blanks in the average MMC published report have grown over time. (Utility regulators are no less bound by the current conventions.) To pursue this line would take us too far afield; no doubt a complex cost-benefit calculation would be argued for. But it should certainly not be ignored, as it was, in the context of reforming competition law.

Penalties and Compensation

Discussions of the Green Paper are much exercised by the perceived need to strengthen financial penalties on the wrong-doer, and to a lesser extent, by the need for the 'victim' of abuse to get financial compensation. These ideas were dropped in Mr Hamilton's statement. It may be that the drafters of the Green Paper were over-impressed by the experience in the Competition Act's operation, which was heavily weighted by the crop of predation cases involving the bus industry. These certainly highlighted the possibility of losses to small entrants via incumbent reaction to entry. They also, however, aptly illustrated the point that alleged predation is difficult not only to demonstrate but that a long time must elapse before the consequences of the conduct complained of can be shown. In particular, in the referred cases, the MMC accepted the OFT's conditions for showing predation, including the critical one that predation must be 'feasible' – that is, shown to be profitable to the incumbent. Predatory behaviour in those cases was, in effect, seen as the incumbent's front-end investment for a later pay-off when, among other things, his reputation for attacking entrants would postpone possible future entry. The trouble is, of course, that in none of the cases was the evidence pushed through to demonstrate the pay-off. This would not only have been extremely difficult to show, but it would in any case have required a much longer history of incumbent action. Meanwhile, the unlucky first entrant might well be pushed towards bankruptcy.[5]

---

[5] One of the further difficulties in these cases was the active possibility that the conduct was supported by the incumbent's exceptionally weak bankruptcy constraint – especially where public owners were the incumbents.

Since the decision was to drop prohibitions, the possibility of fines was dropped too. So was that of compensation for the victim of AMP. In view of my earlier arguments about the conditions for making appropriate judgement, especially ahead of argument before an appellate mechanism, that levying fines was dropped is just as well. One also has to face the objections of principle on the compensation side, namely, that since the essence of capitalism is the possibility of making losses as well as gains, it is wrong to intervene to modify the process. But if one starts with the proposition – as did the Green Paper, which followed a broad consensus – that more should be done to encourage entry (that is, there is not enough challenge to incumbents in general), then it is appropriate to approach the problem of penalties and compensation more fundamentally, through considering profit incentives.

At base, the consensus is that, on the one hand, on the incumbent's side, abuse is not costly enough; on the other, that it would be useful to lower entrants' risks, specifically to hold out better prospects of compensation if failure occurs. I would argue that we wish not to empower regulators to levy penalties as a possibly abusive story unfolds, or to perform the impossible task of assessing what a fine should be in the absence of a direct test of damage caused. We should look to a more general means to do this. As a principle of fairness, it must be applied simultaneously to both sides. So we are led to a system in which aggrieved entrants may sue incumbents for compensation. The appropriate forum is one in which the whole course of conduct can be reviewed, 'guilt' established or not, and judgement made accordingly. Such judgement is clearly a rôle for the courts, and in the UK context, would have to be added to the administrative process in the form I described earlier.

The snag is, of course, that as a deterrent/compensation system the costs and pay-offs to actions for damages are, at any one time, fairly remote. So we are also led to a US-style solution – the possibility of multiple damages. (It would also help the possibly impecunious entrant if cases were to be taken on a no-win-no-fee basis.) I think that the UK's administrative system can very usefully be extended to add this weapon to the pro-competitive armoury. I have in mind that the question of establishing the facts about a case of abuse should, as now, rest with the administrative system, and, in particular, the MMC. An adverse judgement by the MMC in that system, as now, would lead to the formulation of appropriate remedies within the administrative system's scope, and (I would hope) to trenchant opinion about the need for action, including primary legislation, to correct the underlying entry conditions. Also implicit in this judgement will be varying degrees of guilty intent. Quite often, damage is done unwittingly to entrants; often the fault, if any, lies more in the consequences of following constraints imposed exogenously rather than imposed by the incumbent, etc. Any of these may lead to proposed remedies, as they should, without raising the question of culpability.

But many cases do raise the question, of course. This is where MMC judgements are likely to be seen as fair, particularly if, to reach them, the procedures I have suggested are adopted. A critical part of preserving the MMC's reputation for fairness is its manifest independence. It neither triggers nor influences its own involvement, and it has no part in enforcement of its proposed remedies. It was for this reason, mainly, that I viewed with alarm suggestions as the Green Paper was being formulated that the MMC or its members should become involved in a fine-setting process.

The degree of guilt displayed in an adverse MMC judgement should in my view be the central concern of the High Court in which cases following the administrative process could be brought. I have considerable sympathy with the arguments, strongly expressed in the Green Paper discussion, that vexatious proceedings should be avoided. Accordingly, the right to sue should be dependent on the outcome of an adverse finding by the MMC. The Court would always have the prerogative, when a private action is brought, of disagreeing with the precedent administrative judgement, but would be rather unlikely, I judge, to do much second guessing of a thorough report like the MMC's.

Since the train of action following what turns out to be 'guilty' practice is likely to be prolonged, there is a strong case for multiple damages, say to the three-fold level of the USA, if 'guilt' is indeed confirmed by the Court. I also have a suggestion on the Court's problem of assessing the losses to the plaintiff. The damage actually done to a plaintiff in the particular case should be viewed in the context of the plaintiff's net worth. What is established as a cash loss because of the conduct of the incumbent is a disaster to one entrant but a pin-prick to another. So in terms of its ability to pursue further commercial ventures the full triple damages would be payable to the entrant most harmed; simple damages to the least harmed. As this suggestion may well have shown, I am no legal expert. But I *would* claim that it follows the logic of bearing on the problem as a real exercise in commercial incentives. Once the system is going, the possibility of adverse outcomes and compensation will – as in the USA – become a normal part of corporate decision-making. The desired shift towards competition will have been accomplished.

Conclusion

I hope that my own programme for replacing the mouse with a rather more formidable animal will lead to a lively discussion. I have concluded that progress in dealing with AMP depends on improving the present administrative process, while raising the prospective costs of AMP to incumbents, and lowering those to entrants. The MMC should be used more, not less, as in effect now proposed. Its own procedures should be sharpened to shift more of the burden of showing that conduct is not an abuse to the incumbent. More relevant commercial information should be made available. On the most neglected issue – of penalties and compensation – I would like to see private actions to claim up to threefold damages, depending on the degree of culpability disclosed by an MMC investigation. The High Court, in awarding damages, should tailor them to the entrant's lack of means.

But I would like to close by recalling that there has been much discussion recently of the need for the utility regulators to aim to create conditions in their own industries where, having sorted out the problem of natural monopoly control from that of promoting competition, they can yield matters of the control of AMP to the wider competition authorities. My argument, in effect, has been that this will become practicable only when the lessons of their experience have been absorbed, and duly turned into reform of that wider framework.

*   *   *

As a postscript to the lecture and discussion that followed it, I have been persuaded by Sir Sydney Lipworth's comments that in addition to my proposals it would be necessary to change the law in order to create the ground for the High Court's decision. I think this could be accomplished simply by making abuse of monopoly power (with no further specification) as the offence, and providing for the MMC's prior participation in investigating a case as a condition for recognition of an 'abuse'.

CHAIRMAN'S COMMENTS

Sir Sydney Lipworth
Formerly Chairman, Monopolies and Mergers Commission

PROFESSOR BEESLEY HAS GIVEN us a most compelling and fascinating address, and there were a lot of extremely interesting and innovative ideas there. So compelling, in fact, that I found myself almost in agreement! I certainly agree with all those nice things you said about the MMC; I could not have put them better myself. But I think I have to take issue on a number of key points about the type of system you have in mind.

For me, the main questions are, firstly, whether a prohibition and fine-based system can sit easily alongside a public interest, remedies-based monopoly and merger régime. Secondly, I am also not clear – and this is where, perhaps, the economists here can help – how great a need there is for fines and damages as a deterrent and an incentive. And a third very knotty point is, what the legal framework has to be in order to make fines and damages possible.

Let me start off as an advocate of the 'mouse' that you say has emerged. Indeed, I find it a very effective mouse, and I will give my reasons briefly. I was quite surprised when the Green Paper actually came out. It was largely a response to a query that I and others had raised quite early on when changes were first mooted, that if one moved to a system of prohibition in relation to RTP, what would happen to the rest of competition law? Option 2 of the Green Paper would have had the effect that the prohibition system might replace a major part of the MMC's work, so I was rather startled when it emerged, and I was against it. Fortunately, that option has been nailed.

Present System Non-Legalistic

I started off with the fact that the essence of the UK system of monopoly control over the last 45 years is that it is not legalistic and it is not based on prohibition. Indeed, the legislation deliberately eschewed undue legalism and tried, as far as possible, to avoid the Courts. It became logical against that background that the determination of the facts and the effects should be handed over to the findings of an independent commission consisting of individuals from a variety of backgrounds who (and this is the important point) had the right to determine their own procedures and did not function as a Court. Moreover, monopolies are not deemed to be illegal or offensive *per se*. What was relevant was how the public interest was or would be affected. This is still the case.

Option 2, the prohibition system to replace the existing system, would require radical legislation. It would impose a sea-change calling for a much more legalistic system, institutional changes and a system of fines. For the sake of consistency the whole competition area, in my view, not just the monopoly régime, but also mergers, would have to be reviewed. Quite apart from anything else, there would be great practical problems: it would be difficult for such complicated legislation to find a parliamentary slot. Of course, as Professor Beesley points out, that would be a bad reason for not going ahead if there was a very good case for such a system. But I think the legislative problems are a fact of life we have to face.

Option 3 is an uneasy halfway house. It would have a prohibition which, although it would be an add-on to the existing system, would still require a philosophical change, and would still require a change in the way of operating. It would also need radical legislation, although far less, and, again, I think it would have been quite unlikely to get a parliamentary slot at an early stage. With Option 3, which route would you take? Would you apply the Article 86 equivalent or go through the existing procedures?

But behind it all really lies the first question: Is there a compelling case for a prohibition, even if it is only tagged on to the present system? My starting point here is that any investigation of monopoly power and abuse, whether under the present system or under any of the options, can be divided into two parts. The first part, obviously, is the investigation of the facts that give rise to the possible concerns, and the second part is to look at the potential remedies or penalties if the facts justify action.

FTA and Competition Act Provisions Adequate – Prohibition Not Required

Now, as far as the initial investigation is concerned, the provisions of the Fair Trading Act, coupled with the Competition Act, are, at the very least, adequate enough without any prohibition to cover all types of predatory and other conduct that are contemplated by Article 86.

Indeed, if we look through all the MMC monopoly and Competition Act cases, virtually every one of the illustrative items of conduct, both in the courts and in the Commission rulings, and in Article 86 itself, have been covered at some time or other by the MMC under the Fair Trading Act. But the Fair Trading Act, in fact, goes much further. The sections encompass not only conduct, but also the very structure of the situation itself; the OFT not only examines abuse, but it also looks at the potential for abuse. The thresholds are far lower than the Article 86-type thresholds; they are flexible enough to include single monopolists, or more than one with collective shares of over 25 per cent, so the question of joint dominance does not present any problems. My thesis is that you do not need any prohibition in order to get an investigation as often as you want and whenever you want.

As far as the present remedies are concerned, they are there, basically, to correct the adverse effects in the future. The system does not start off with any presumptions. The types of order that are possible under the Fair Trading Act may fall short of fines, but in many respects, they go very much further. There is a much wider range of penalties or remedies than under Article 86: divestment, price controls, publication of information, alteration of contractual terms, prohibitions on behaviour, and so on. I would also question whether the deterrence is as weak as has been suggested.

Looking back over the cases the MMC has had in the last five to seven years, I can think of very few that were not adequately covered by the remedies available and where fines or damages would have been preferable. In one or two, in fact, we did suggest that other remedies would be desirable. These were mainly the rather unrepresentative bus cases where there was a particular form of predatory conduct and a rather slow procedure under the legislation to stop it, which is now addressed by the Green Paper.

So the proposed amendments are helpful. The Competition Act did need toughening, and we pointed that out in a number of our reports. I think that interim relief goes a very long way to achieving that. What it boils down to is that, if there is abuse of conduct and a complaint, the new orders or the new rules will enable either the DGFT or the Secretary of State, however the legislation is drawn, to grant in effect an interim injunction. Now that need not be the terribly serious thing that Professor Beesley suggested; in the same way as an injunction anywhere, it can be done on a balance of convenience at that stage, pending a fairly short-term investigation by the MMC. The proposed undertakings which would avert a Competition Act investigation or monopolies reference do have teeth because they can be buttressed by an enforceable order.

Are Fines/Triple Fines a Deterrent?

So, in my view, there is enough there without looking for prohibition and fines. But on the very innovative and, I think, in some ways appealing suggestions for fines and triple fines, one has to ask, first, is this *necessary* as a *deterrent*? Is there evidence that the fines and prohibitions system of the EEC and other member-states has produced a very much more competitive environment than the UK? But even assuming it has, I have other difficulties with the suggestion. The suggested use of the MMC as the final or virtually final arbiter of the facts is novel and *prima facie* attractive. Traditionally, it fits in well with the MMC's work and, of course, I would personally welcome a greater use of the MMC.

But the lawyer in me steps in at this point: How do you achieve a right to damages and a duty on which a fine can be pegged? In my view, the only way you can do that is to base it on some statutory duty and statutory right, which means a prohibition and very detailed legislation, particularly if we were to follow Michael's suggestion of shifting the burden of proof and going for triple damages. So we are really back full circle again to Option 2/Option 3 and all the problems they raise. I do not see how you can get that system in place without some very detailed and radical legislation.

Also, if the MMC is to be the vehicle for the ultimate decision that results in fines and damages, this could compromise the present co-operative atmosphere that it relies on in its current procedures. Private interests will now be involved and at stake and, very soon, there will be hostile adversarial and legal procedures. I think that is something one would live with if, in fact, the gain was commensurate. There would also need to be a right of appeal, which you do not have at the moment; now, there is judicial review only. And the present system's speed and reasonable finality would be casualties. Third parties do have some safeguards now, in the sense of breach of orders giving rise to action, and of course interim relief to stop abuse will be available in the future. So, I would open for discussion the question of whether Michael's starting point is right, that there is a great benefit to be gained from somehow moving the system to allow for fines and penalties.

On the MMC's and others' use of commercially sensitive material, in the MMC's case there are a lot more blanks because there are also a lot more words in our reports, but, nonetheless, I think the UK is, perhaps, a little bit over-sensitive. Many things that are done quite openly in the United States are not done here, but that is something one would want to get more of a general consensus on.

Finally, shifting the burden of proof, even under the current system, would be a remarkably difficult step, in my view, and would require, again, legislative change. I am not sure that it would be a step in the right direction.